FLY THE AIRPLANE!

A Retired Pilot's Guide to Fight Safety
For Pilots, Present and Future

CHARLES WOOD

GACHONG Press

Copyright ©2022 Charles Wood

Editor-in-Chief Lynda Alexander

Print ISBN: 978-1-66785-785-5

eBook ISBN: 978-1-66785-786-2

Cover art by James Gillette, grandson of my best friend Les Shobe (1935-2019).

James, you made Pop-Pop proud!

James and Pop-Pop, 2013

Final cover design magic by my son Robert Wood. Thanks Robert!

Thanks to my daughter Kathryn Wood for doing a "totally unnecessary" final text review before I sent it to the publisher. She found five major blunders I had made that no proof-reader or editor could have noticed. Kate, you are Awesome!

Many thanks to my friend Captain Douglas Moss for bringing this book up to date regarding modern technology that has come into being since I retired. I wanted to make sure that nobody has invented a new gadget that negates a pilot's responsibility to FLY THE AIRPLANE. Doug has assured me that no one has.

Extra special thanks to my nephew Shawn Taylor, who read the early manuscript of this book just as he was beginning to train for his pilot license. His observations about how the FLY THE AIRPLANE!

philosophy influenced his pre-solo, solo and post-solo attitude toward flight safety have shown me that writing this book was a worthwhile effort.

For most of my 45-year flying career, I have been a student of flight safety. I feel that learning from other people's mistakes has been one of the main reasons that I have over 20,000 accident-free flying hours.

I have been trying for years to put into words what I have learned so I could share them with other pilots. The inspiration for this book started several years ago with a conversation I had with a couple of my Japanese friends I had previously trained in the MD-90. Captain Shosuke Ando and Captain Tadashi Hasegawa from Japan Air System airline visited my wife and me for two days in 2015. The first evening we got into a long conversation about flying. My wife excused herself at about 10pm, and our conversation continued until after midnight. I was talking to Captain Ando about when you fly a glider or sailplane, that is what you must do: FLY THE AIRPLANE. It suddenly dawned on me that those three words explain why I have 45 years of accident-free flying! Thank you, Ando san and Hasegawa san!

This book was written for pilots: People who want to be pilots, people training to be pilots, recreational pilots, military pilots, people beginning careers as pilots and even "Old Timer" pilots.

This should be required reading for airplane designers and design engineers.

The title of this book "FLY THE AIRPLANE!" should be permanently imbedded in every pilot's brain, to be the overriding thought any time the pilot is in the cockpit during flight.

These three words may seem redundant if you are a pilot flying solo, but they are NOT!

And any time you are with another pilot in the cockpit of an airplane with dual flight controls, that should be the thought that makes the difference between life and death.

During my 45-year flying career, I have seen hundreds of times where NO ONE WAS FLYING THE AIRPLANE. In most of these instances the flight continued without problem; But in too many cases, it caused a fatal crash.

There is another phrase called "Loss of situational awareness" that is the same as "No one is flying the airplane". This phenomenon frequently results in what is called "Controlled Flight into Terrain (CFIT)" accidents.

In the following pages I will show you why you must make FLY THE AIRPLANE something you don't have to think about – it is something you automatically MUST DO!

Charlie Wood

Charlie Wood enlisted in the U.S. Air Force after high school graduation and became an airplane engine mechanic. After 2 years he was accepted as an Aviation Cadet, and after pilot/officer training graduated as a Second Lieutenant and Pilot.

He flew world-wide transport aircraft missions including the Vietnam War, was stationed in Japan, Georgia, the Philippines, Spain, Germany, and Illinois. He flew C-124, C-141, C-54, T-39, and C-9 aircraft. He obtained an FAA pilots license with endorsements for Instructor, Glider, and Airline Transport Pilot. He also flew Piper Cub, Cessna single engine, and qualified in Schweizer, Schleicher and Blanik sailplanes.

As a civilian pilot at Douglas, McDonnell Douglas, and Boeing, he flew experimental and production test flights, and trained airline pilots in the U.S., Yugoslavia, Mexico, France, Germany, Singapore, Argentina, Taiwan, China, and Japan. He flew DC-9, MD-80, MD-90, DC-10, MD-11 and B-717 aircraft. He qualified in the Aero Commander airplane.

He retired with over 20,000 accident-free flying hours. In this book, the 83-year-old pilot shares what he learned about safe flying during his 45-year flying career.

This book is a must read for student pilots, and based on recent airplane accidents, needs to be read by all active pilots, airplane manufacturers and design engineers.

CONTENTS

CHAPTER 1:

AVIATION HISTORY

THE EARLY YEARS

The first FLY THE AIRPLANE incident probably went like this: A two-seat biplane makes a hard landing on a grass airstrip, ground-loops and ends up upside-down. The dust clears, both pilots grope their way out of their seats, and then blame each other for the terrible landing. They both thought that the other pilot was flying the airplane. NO ONE WAS!

In the early days of aviation before anyone could even spell CFIT (Controlled Flight into Terrain), it was easy to get lost and run into something. Airplanes started out as being not much more than kites with engines. The brave souls who flew them took their lives in their hands every time they strapped themselves in.

By the way, that "strap" was an afterthought that resulted from some poor pilot who fell to his death because he either rolled his craft upside down or pulled negative "Gs" then realized that he wasn't attached to his airplane. As he plummeted to the ground, the last words he said were most likely "Oh S...t!" ... these have been the last words of many pilots.

Up until the late 1930s, when you flew an airplane, you had to see where you were going because all you had for navigation were your eyes. You really had to be careful to stay out of any clouds, rain, smoke, or fog. Many a pilot inadvertently flew into worsening weather, lost sense of up and down, and either went into a graveyard spiral into the ground or hit something (like a mountain).

BACK THEN

There were no aviation maps, so if you couldn't see familiar landmarks you were lost. If you got lost but were smart enough to stay out of the weather and mountainous terrain, the best thing you could do was FLY THE AIRPLANE. There were usually plenty of cornfields you could put down in before you ran out of gas. Then, if Farmer Jones didn't shoot you before you could ask him where the heck you were, you might be able to find out how to get back to where you came from.

NO MATTER WHAT HAPPENS

FLY THE AIRPLANE

WORLD WAR I

The first war birds were a quantum leap from the original airplanes. They were faster, more maneuverable, had more range and altitude capabilities. Some, such as the Spad, Fokker and Jenny were a joy to fly.

But if you got into weather, you immediately lost track of where you were. If you were lucky enough to be able to keep your wings level, you now had the capability to hit a higher mountain at a higher speed.

Spad – French fighter biplane

AIRMAIL

In the 1930s airplanes had improved to the point that they could be flown cross-country, with refueling stops every few hundred miles. The first cross-country air service was the U.S. Mail. Brave pilots were hired to fly mail from coast to coast, vastly reducing the time it took to get a letter from point "A" to point "B". Sometimes. Maybe.

Douglas Air Mail Airplane 1926

AIRWAY BEACONS

Airway Beacon

The first "airways" were established using lighthouse-style beacons, to guide the pilot between refueling stops.

Airway maps were published showing airports and towns enroute. Most towns had their names painted in large letters on a predominant water tower or roof so pilots could figure out where they were.

Town Sign

"BLIND" FLIGHT

Rudimentary flight instruments were developed to help pilots keep the wings level in the clouds. Basic instrument flying techniques were developed by trial and error. But again, at night or in the clouds there were still the mountains that frequently got in the way. They never announced their presence until you hit them. Quite a few pilots did.

Jimmy Doolittle "Blind Flight", 1929

RADIO COMMUNICATIONS?

Companies started using primitive voice radio communications to keep track of their airplanes. The radios didn't work very well. They operated on the High Frequency (HF) band and were frequently disrupted by atmospheric conditions.

One company was trying to locate a pilot and established weak radio contact with him. The dispatcher repeatedly asked him to state his position and altitude, and the pilot replied that the transmission was garbled. Out of frustration the dispatcher shouted, "How high are you and where are you?" The pilot replied, "I'm five foot two and I'm in the front of the airplane! ".

RADIO RANGE STATIONS

The range stations were placed along the airways so that the steady tone beams were on the airway course.

To use the range station, the pilot tuned in the station and maneuvered the airplane so that only a steady tone was heard. For instance, if the pilot was flying up the lower right-hand leg of the station and heard a steady tone, he would turn the airplane to a heading of 330 If he heard an A in Morse code, it meant that he needed to turn left to get back on course. Simple? No! Because if he was headed away from the station on the upper left-hand leg and heard an A, it meant that he had to turn right to get back on course.

So, another complexity appeared in the equation - the pilot had to listen if the signal was getting stronger or weaker, to tell whether he was going towards or away from the station. Try to do that in an open cockpit, with the wind and engine noise drowning out the radio station signal! It was hard enough in an airplane where you can hear the signal clearly.

I sincerely believe that whoever invented the Radio Range Approach was trying to distract pilots from FLYING THE AIRPLANE by making them think about N's and A's, and volume increasing or decreasing, and which direction to turn.

It was a very difficult thing to do, and I'm glad nobody in the world must fly a Radio Range Approach anymore. The last Radio Range station was decommissioned in the late 1960s.

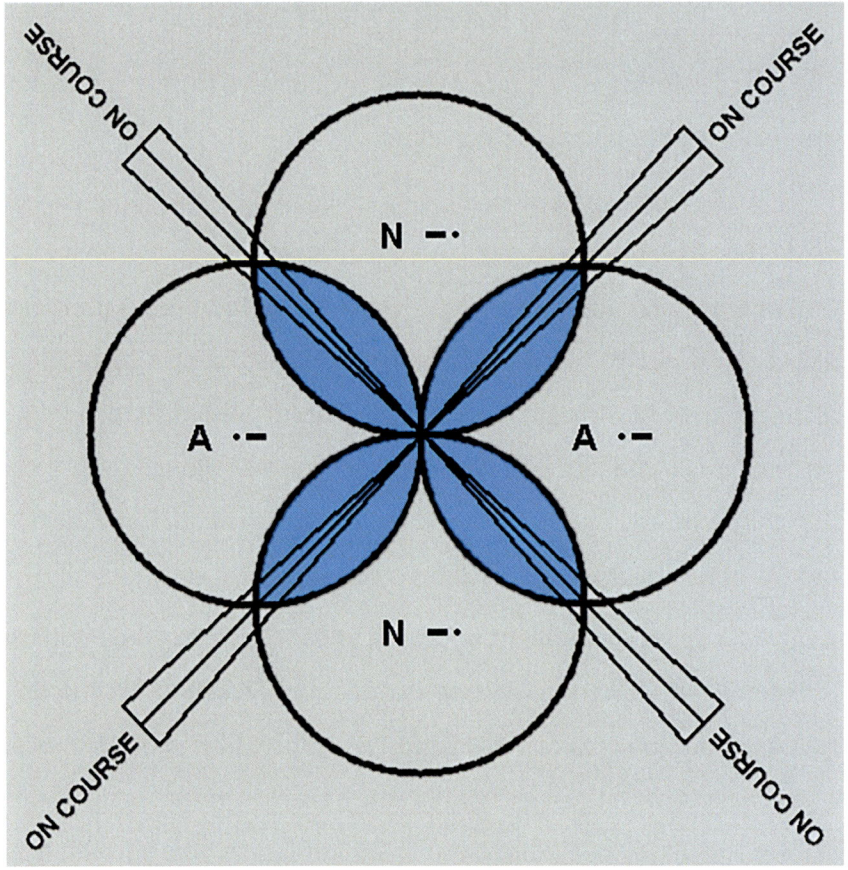

Radio Range Station

I was a 22-year-old First Lieutenant with just over 1,500 hours in the Douglas C-124 Globemaster II when I upgraded to Aircraft Commander. The final part of my check ride was flying a simulated 2 engines-out Radio Range Approach into Tachikawa Air Base, Japan. That was probably the most difficult instrument approach I have ever flown.

C-124 Aircraft Commander 1st Lieutenant Charles Wood
Air Force Times Photo

NON-DIRECTIONAL BEACONS (NDB)

One of the greatest advances in navigation was the Non-Directional Beacon (NDB). NDBs also broadcast in the AM band in an omni directional signal. Pilots flying aircraft equipped with an Automatic Direction Finder (ADF) receiver could tune in the station, and an instrument in the cockpit would point a needle to the station. The instrument had a compass on it, so the pilot could maneuver the airplane to track any course to or from the station.

This was a great improvement except that the ADF needle was more inclined to point to thunderstorms than the station. Many pilots ran into mountains homing in on thunderstorms. They thought they knew where they were going, but ...

ADF

WORLD WAR II

WWII placed a demand on aviators to fly and fight with varying levels of experience, in a vast variety of airplanes and all kinds of weather.

TALK ABOUT "FLY THE AIRPLANE!"

My favorite FLY THE AIRPLANE story is about a Nashville boy named Robert Hoover who learned how to fly in 1937. To overcome an airsickness problem, he taught himself how to do aerobatics.

In WW II Robert enlisted in the Tennessee National Guard and was sent to U.S. Army Air Force Aviation Cadet program for pilot training. On his first flight as a student pilot, he showed his instructor a maneuver that wasn't in the syllabus – an 8-point aileron roll. After landing Robert's instructor told his commander "I refuse to fly with Hoover anymore because he knows more about flying than I do!"

After he graduated from Aviation Cadets, 20-year-old Flight Officer Hoover was sent to Casablanca, Morocco. Because of his demonstrated piloting skills, he was assigned as a Test Pilot to fly the first flight of repaired war-damaged fighter planes and newly assembled warplanes.

Flight Officer Robert Hoover

Test flying the repaired planes was not usually a problem, but the flying the newly assembled planes was something else. They had been shipped to Morocco in crates and were assembled by a ragtag mixture of Army Air corps mechanics and locally hired mechanics who may or not have been able to read English language assembly instructions. Hoover flew as many as 12 test flights a day, and quickly learned that to FLY THE AIRPLANE, the AIRPLANE must first be FLYABLE.

Most of the newly assembled planes had safety-of-flight problems: Critical parts missing, fuel or oil leaks, or the flight controls were mis-rigged. After a few near-fatal inflight incidents requiring every bit of his innate ability to FLY THE AIRPLANE, Hoover quickly learned to get these problems fixed before flight, so they didn't become inflight emergencies.

Many of the new planes had assembly problems that were not detectable on the ground and resulted in engine failure during the flight. Hoover learned how to be a glider pilot without ever flying a glider. Perhaps that was the point in his flying career that he coined the term "Energy Management": To FLY THE AIRPLANE, you must make sure that the airplane has enough ENERGY to perform what you want to do (such as make a safe landing).

In an airplane, energy consists of Airspeed, Altitude, Thrust and Ideas. The most important of these forms of energy is altitude; because if you run out of altitude the other three things can't help you. If you successfully manage an airplane's energy, you are FLYING THE AIRPLANE!

NOTE: If you didn't recognize who I have been talking about here, this guy was the late Bob Hoover (1922-2016), in my opinion the best AIRPLANE FLYER the world has ever seen. He did things with a twin engine Aero Commander that were amazing: He performed a perfect 1G barrel roll while pouring iced tea into a glass without spilling a drop.

In his Energy Management Finale, he made a high-speed low pass over the runway, pulled up into a 45° climb while feathering both engines, performed an aileron roll, did a 180° turn, landed on the opposite runway, touching down first on one main landing gear wheel then the other, and still had enough energy remaining to taxi right up to his parking spot in front of the audience!

WARTIME IMPROVEMENTS TO HELP YOU FLY BETTER

Manufacturers developed improved flight instruments such as the gyro horizon - a device that showed the pilot the pitch and bank of the airplane most of the time (The gyros were primitive and tended to tumble if you made a violent maneuver or display an erroneous reading due to bearing friction - your wings could be level and the gyro would indicate you were doing something else.

Erroneous Gyro Horizon Display

Bombers and transport airplanes were capable of interconti-nental flight and carried navigators. Navigators were trained to use celestial navigation and "dead reckoning".

CELESTIAL NAVIGATION

Celestial navigation required that the navigator be able to see the stars or sun and use a sextant to plot the position of the airplane. A good navigator could determine the airplane's position within several miles by taking a three star "shot" and triangulating this data onto a map.

If the navigator mistakenly shot the wrong star or another airplane's navigational lights (it has happened!), all bets were off.

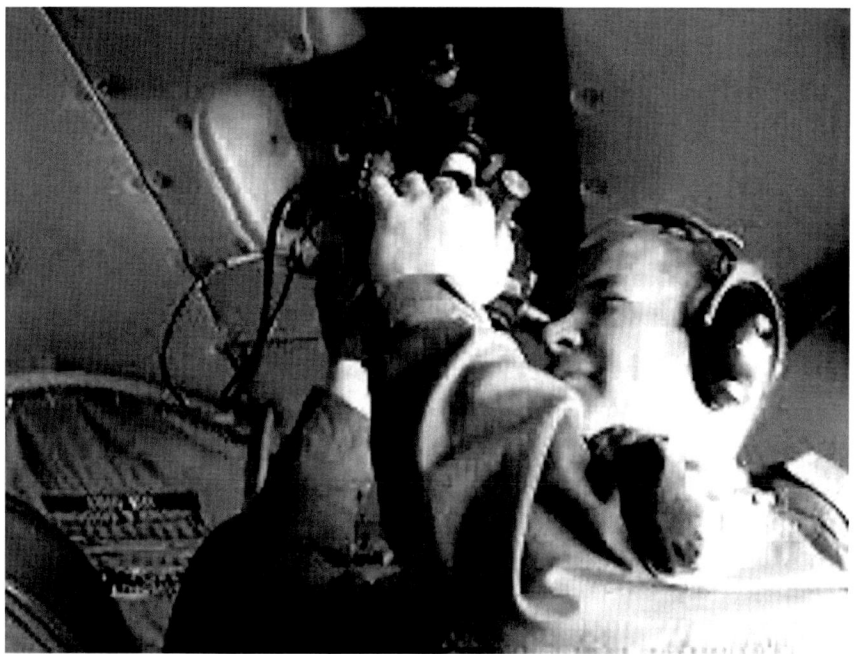

Airborne celestial "shot"

DEAD RECKONING

Dead reckoning is an educated guess as to where the airplane is located, based on time, airspeed, altitude, forecast winds, observed drift and last known position. Weather forecasting was not good in those days, and many airplanes were blown way off course by un-forecasted winds and ended up ditching in the ocean or crash landing in remote areas. Dead reckoning was frequently just that.

EVOLUTION OF RADAR

Radar was originally developed as a device to provide early warning of enemy air attacks. Later it was refined to become the most sophisticated device ever for determining an airplane's location.

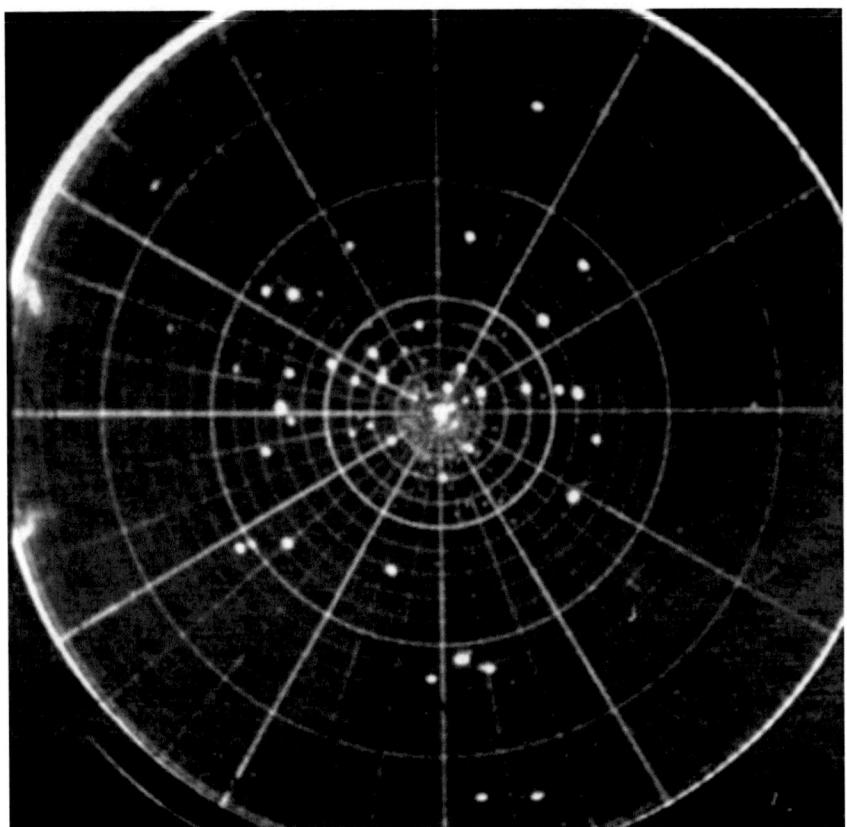

Early Radar screen

GROUND CONTROLLED APPROACH (GCA)

Radar operators on the ground could talk to pilots on the radio and tell them exactly where they were. Some airfields had Ground Controlled Approach (GCA) radars allowing radar operators to "talk airplanes down" in bad weather.

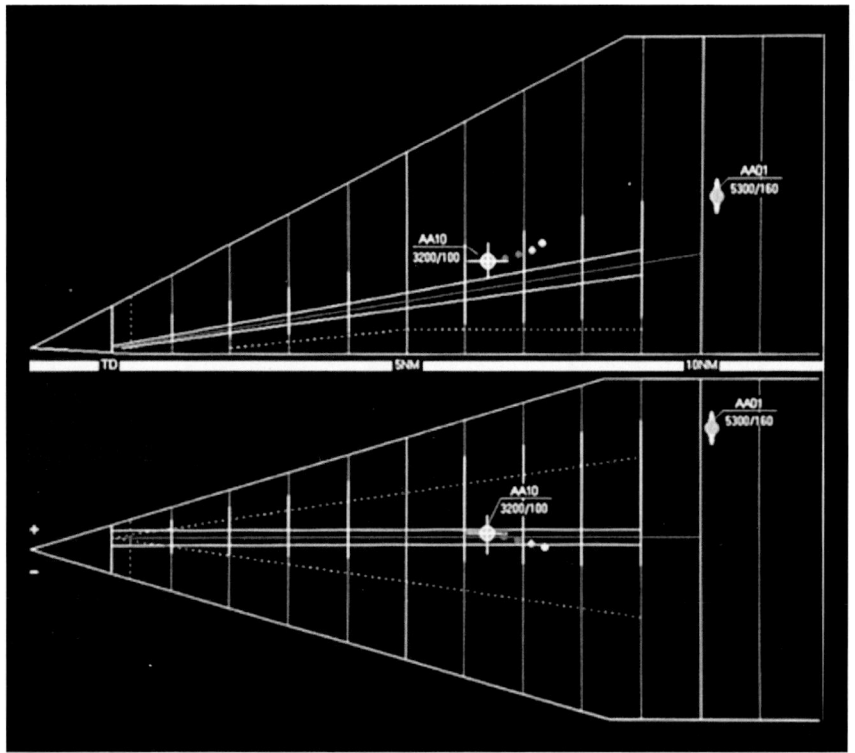

GCA Controller's Radar Display

When I was a very young pilot, a GCA Controller not only showed me how important it is to FLY THE AIRPLANE; This guy saved my life as well as the lives of my crew and passengers:

"DON'T BEAM ME UP SCOTTY – TALK ME DOWN!" MY GCA STORY

I was on a night flight from Tachikawa, Japan to Clark AFB, Philippines. Weather was forecast to be clear for our arrival time at Clark. The C-124 was loaded to the maximum takeoff weight of 175,000 pounds. Because of the good weather forecast, we only carried the minimum reserve of fuel. We used a large amount of our reserve fuel enroute, diverting around thunderstorms. That was ok because the Philippines were forecasted to have clear skies.

When we got within radio range of Clark, we were informed that a fog bank had rolled in, and every airport within our fuel range was socked in, including Clark. I had no choice. I HAD to land at Clark. We were radar vectored to fly a Ground Controlled Approach (GCA), the only "precision" approach available at Clark that night.

A GCA is an approach where you are talked down by an approach controller called anOperator. The GCA Operator monitors your position and altitude on a radar screen. The operator talks you down by telling you to turn this way or that, and to increase or decrease or maintain your descent rate. If you don't have visual contact when you are 200 feet above the ground, you must abort the approach and initiate a climb (Go Around).

GCA operator reflected in his radar screen

I flew the GCA as instructed by this great controller. He talked me through a perfect approach and kept me exactly on course and glide slope. When I reached 200 feet, I didn't see the runway, so I applied maximum power on the engines and started a climb. Just as I pulled the nose up, I caught sight of the runway lights, but that was too late to safely pull the power off and land. My fuel state was now critical. I didn't have enough fuel to go to Cubi Point or Manila (the weather at those airports was bad anyway). I HAD to land!

The Controller talked me through another perfect approach, and when I reached 200 feet he said, "Do you have the runway in sight?" I replied, "Keep talking!" He did. I saw the runway lights at about 100 feet. I landed safely thanks to his expertise. When I turned off the runway, the visibility was so bad I couldn't taxi to the parking spot. I stopped on the taxiway, and told the Command Post we needed to be towed in. It took the tow driver 30 minutes to find us in the fog.

God Bless that GCA Controller!

CHAPTER 2:

POST- WAR YEARS

AIRLINE GROWTH

Commercial aviation grew in leaps and bounds after the end of WW II. Surplus military airplanes were converted into airliners:

The venerable C-47 "Gooney Bird" was the DC-3

The C-54 Skymaster was the DC-4

The B-29 / B-50 turned into the luxurious pressurized B-377 Stratocruiser

The C-118 was a DC-6

The C-121 Lockheed Constellation became the pride of Trans World Airways.

Boeing, Lockheed, and Douglas Aircraft companies thrived.

NAVIGATIONAL AID IMPROVEMENTS

Airplanes were still running into mountains because pilots couldn't always tell exactly where they were during a flight. This led pilot unions and airlines to demand new devices that would help pilots determine their position (Know where you are = FLY THE AIRPLANE).

VERY HIGH FREQUENCY OMNIDIRECTIONAL RANGE (VOR)

The Very high frequency Omnidirectional Range (VOR) station was a great improvement. The ground station operated in the VHF band and sent out an accurate signal up to about 100 miles, depending on the altitude of the airplane and terrain. The aircraft receiver had a compass and a needle that pointed to the station (Like the old ADF receiver), plus the pilot had another instrument where the precise course to or from the station could be set in the Course Deviation Indicator (CDI).

This course could be maintained by centering a vertical bar on the instrument. Since VOR stations operated in the VHF range, the needles were not affected by thunderstorms.

VOR CDI

VOR AIRWAYS

In the United States VOR airways were established, and airways maps were published showing the routes between stations, station frequencies and minimum enroute altitudes. Air Traffic Control radars and voice radio stations were installed in many parts of the country, which insured an orderly flow of air traffic.

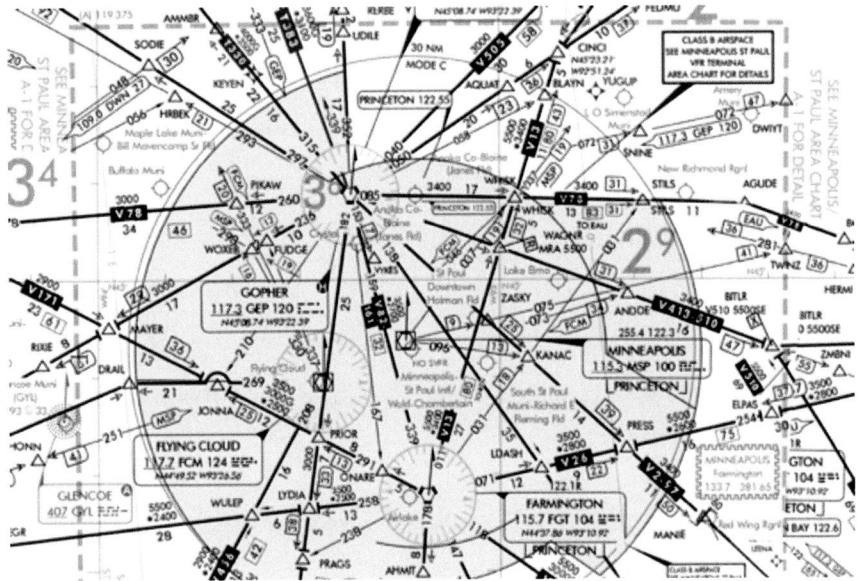

Jeppesen Chart

The rest of the world was slow to catch up with the U.S., and until the late 1960s most of the airways outside the U.S. were at best the old NDB stations. In some countries airways were nonexistent - dead reckoning was the name of the game. Uncharted mountains frequently got in the way of unlucky aviators.

LONG RANGE NAVIGATION (LORAN)

Over water navigation capabilities improved with the advent of Long-Range Navigation (LORAN) stations. These stations were in numerous places all over the world and broadcast a long-range navigational signal. Navigators could tune these stations and be able to plot an aircraft position sometimes accurate to within a few miles. I say sometimes because LORAN signals can be adversely affected by atmospheric conditions.

INSTRUMENT LANDING SYSTEM (ILS)

One of the greatest improvements in landing navigational aids was the Instrument Landing System (ILS). The ground transmitter sent a course and glide path signal from the landing runway, and the aircraft receiver had an instrument that showed the pilot the location of the airplane relative to the course and glide path. This new capability allowed the pilot to find the runway and land the airplane in weather as low as a 200-foot cloud base and 1/2-mile visibility.

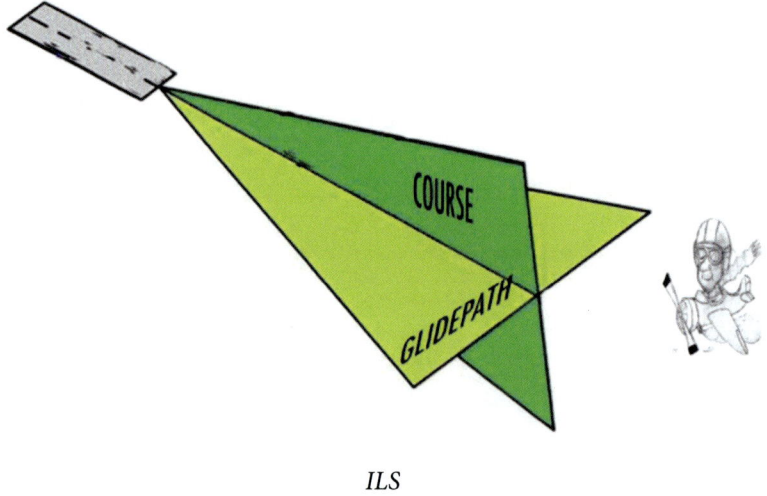

ILS

DISTANCE MEASURING EQUIPMENT (DME)

Distance Measuring Equipment (DME) started being installed on some VOR and ILS transmitters and receivers.

This was a great improvement, for now pilots could know not only where they were relative to or from a station, but also how far from the station they were. This is what they used to figure out where they were: Knowing where you are is one of the most important things you must know to be able to FLY THE AIRPLANE!

VOR/DME

CHAPTER 3:

THE JET AGE

Most of the bad weather in the world is below an altitude of 25,000 feet.

Until the advent of jet airliners, most of the propeller-powered airplanes were unpressurized, and were restricted to cruise altitudes below 10,000 feet. The pressurized planes such as the Stratocruiser, DC-6 and DC-7 could struggle up to altitudes around 18,000 feet. You could expect a rough ride on a long flight. A lot of that went away when the jet came of age.

The early jet airliners, the Boeing 707, the Douglas DC-8 and the Convair 880, were noisy - but they were fast, and they cruised at 35,000-40,000 feet. You were assured of a smooth ride over the bad weather below except when the pilot inadvertently got into the invisible Clear Air Turbulence (CAT) associated with the jet stream.

The jet stream is a core of high-speed wind that travels generally from West to East This small tube of air sometimes contains wind more than 150 miles per hour within it, while the winds surrounding it are very light. When an airplane flies into the jet stream, the shear caused by the difference in wind velocities is what causes CAT.

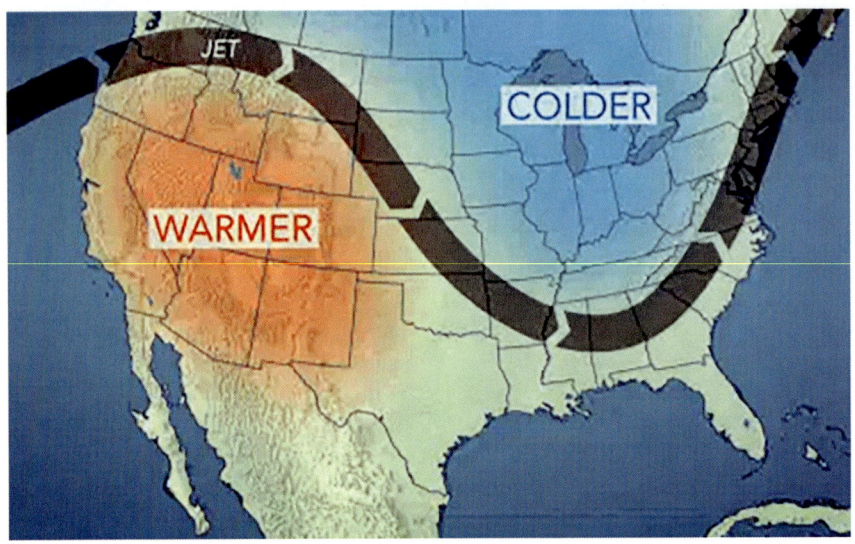

Jet Stream

SAFETY IMPROVEMENTS

Besides being able to fly over most of the weather, the new jetliners were steadily improved as new equipment came on the market, making it easier for you to safely FLY THE AIRPLANE:

- Anti-skid brakes became standard equipment. This greatly improved braking performance on rejected takeoffs and wet/icy runways.

- Cabin environmental systems were improved so that when the airplane is cruising at 35,000 feet with an outside air temperature of -40° to -70°F the cabin pressure is a comfortable 5,000 - 6,000 feet and the cabin temperature is a comfortable 72°F.

- The old unreliable rubber deicing boots were replaced with pneumatically or electrically heated wings and tail.

- Color weather radar became a great aid in avoiding heavy precipitation, hail and severe turbulence associated with thunderstorms

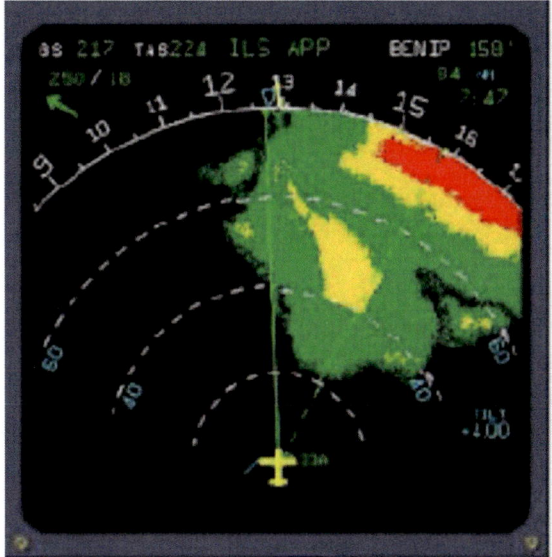

Color radar screen

These are the improvements that more usefully help you safely FLY THE AIRPLANE. But there were still too many accidents being attributed to human error.

CREW RESOURCE MANAGEMENT (CRM)

Accidents most often are attributed to human error; In many cases the "human error" was that nobody was FLYING THE AIRPLANE. The reasons no one was FLYING THE AIRPLANE varied:

- Distracted while troubleshooting landing gear malfunction, a United Airlines DC-8 crew failed to monitor fuel quantity. All four engines flamed out due to fuel starvation and the airplane crashed in a housing area, killing 11 people.

- An Eastern Airlines L1011 crew got distracted troubleshooting a burnt-out light bulb in the landing gear indicating system. None of the 3 pilots in the cockpit noticed that the autopilot went into the descent mode, nor did they respond to the aural "ALTITUDE" warning when the airplane descended 250 feet below the assigned altitude of 2,000feet. The airplane descended into the Everglades National Park swamp, killing everyone on board.

- Numerous airliner crashes were attributed to longtime airline culture of making the captain some sort of God, whose word was law. No one on the crew dared question the CAPTAIN even if the captain was obviously doing something wrong. This was a holdover from the old nautical "The Captain is the Master of His Ship" tradition. This doesn't work so well when your "ship" is travelling almost at the speed of sound.

Finally, some people discovered that there might be ways to alter flight crew behavior patterns to prevent these types of accidents.

The term Cockpit Resource Management (CRM) was coined to describe training courses that were developed to first make sure that someone is always designated to FLY THE AIRPLANE. This person is to be called, believe it or not, the Pilot Flying (PF). The PF's only job is to FLY THE AIRPLANE. The person designated Pilot Not Flying (PNF) is responsible for everything else: checklists, radio calls and all other flight deck duties that might detract from FLYING

THE AIRPLANE. The term PNF was later changed to PM (Pilot Monitoring) to emphasize the non-flying pilot's primary duty – to monitor what the PF was doing.

United Airlines was the first to develop CRM classroom courses. The definition of CRM later became Crew Resource Management, and resulted in improved interaction between the flight deck, cabin crew, Dispatch and Maintenance.

CRM training created a much safer inflight environment. It encouraged better communications in the airplane.

Inexperienced copilots are encouraged by a senior captain to speak up if they see the captain doing something that is questionable.

Cockpit crew members treat cabin crew members with the dignity they deserve as essential crew members responsible for passenger safety in flight and on the ground.

CRM training has probably been the most successful human engineering breakthrough and has become a standard flight crew training subject for airlines worldwide.

CRM is also being taught in military airlift squadrons and any unit where an aircraft has a multi-member crew.

One aspect of CRM should apply to every pilot in the world: FLY THE AIRPLANE! During my time as a Line Training Pilot for a major airplane manufacturer, I experienced quite a few examples of why CRM training should be mandatory to change the habits of the old "Captain is God" philosophy.

I immediately think of one assignment. These are my notes about the assignment:

AN EXAMPLE OF CREW RESOURCE MIS-MANAGEMENT

Air Xxxxxx was a good assignment. We operated out of Paris Orly Airport. My wife Judy and two of the other instructor's wives came to Paris, and we stayed at a Paris Hilton Hotel that was within a few blocks from the Eiffel Tower.

Line Training went well except for one Captain who I will call RB. RB was my student in both simulator and flight training. RB thought he was God's gift to aviation – he was not! In simulator training he didn't want to go by the book, so I wouldn't give him a passing grade until he did it right.

During line training on passenger flights, he wouldn't allow the copilot to question him if he made a mistake – he was the CAPTAIN (THAT is an accident waiting to happen!)

I could write a book about the number of accidents caused by the "Captain is God" philosophy. Because of that dangerous way of thinking, we now teach Crew Resource Management (CRM), where each cockpit crew member is required to speak out if they notice any deviation from standard procedures.

RB was extremely rude to the Flight Attendants, and they were so cowed by his arrogance they refused to communicate with the cockpit. Because of his behavior, I gave him a Fail grade as a Captain. One of the other instructor pilots on our team gave him additional line training and passed him as a Captain. I thought that would be the last time I would hear about RB. I was wrong.

About a year later, I saw the Air Xxxxxx Chief Pilot at Long Beach. He asked me "Did you hear what happened to RB?" The Chief

Pilot told me that one day as he was on the way to work, and he saw an Air Xxxxxx MD-80 on final approach to Orly The airplane was extremely high, then he noticed that the pilot had deployed both thrust reversers in flight (strictly prohibited, and extremely dangerous), and went into a steep dive to get closer to the glide path. The airplane made a hard landing about halfway down the runway.

The Chief Pilot told me that he rushed to the office to see who was flying the airplane; it was RB. The Chief Pilot said he immediately demoted RB to First Officer; due to Pilot Union politics, RB couldn't be fired.

A short time later I was told that RB had killed himself doing aerobatics in a single engine sport plane. They said it wasn't suicide; RB just demonstrated what an incompetent pilot he was.

Thank God he wasn't flying an MD-80!

CHAPTER 4:

THE SPACE AGE

SPACE SPIN-OFFS

The space program has had a profound impact on nearly everything. Most of the technological breakthroughs in the last 70 years are either directly or indirectly related to the space program:

- Electronic miniaturization required to put a craft into space has resulted in things such as digital watches, small radios, television sets, x-ray machines, heart pacemakers, hearing aids, laptop computers, electronic modules that control everything from microwave ovens to the environment in a large skyscraper building, and many more things.

- Laser technology has caused breakthroughs in surgery, precision building, sound reproduction and inertial navigation.

- Global Positioning Satellites (GPS) have been put in orbit. People with a hand-held GPS receiver can now determine their position anywhere on earth to within a couple of feet!

AIRPLANE IMPROVEMENTS

Avoidance Systems (TCAS), fly-by-wire, automatic systems controllers, and many other things that either make flying safer, more reliable or reduce cockpit workload.

Laser gyros have greatly improved the accuracy of inertial navigation platforms. Instead of a heavy failure-prone mechanical gyroscope as its core, the laser inertial navigation system has only one moving part - a piezoelectric dither motor (don't ask me what the heck that is - I think it vibrates the platform so that the laser beams don't collide with each other). The result is that laser gyros drift much less than their mechanical counterparts, giving the pilot a much more accurate position.

"GLASS" COCKPITS

Glass cockpits are installed in most modern airplanes. The information displayed to the pilot is much the same as was displayed in the older airplanes, but it is usually presented in a much easier to use format.

Boeing 787 Cockpit

For instance, information previously shown on instruments scattered all over the cockpit (the attitude indicator, altimeter, airspeed indicator, vertical velocity indicator, radio groundspeed, VOR/ILS course indicator, and flight guidance mode annunciator) is neatly shown on a large Liquid Crystal Display (LCD), the Primary Flight Display (PFD).

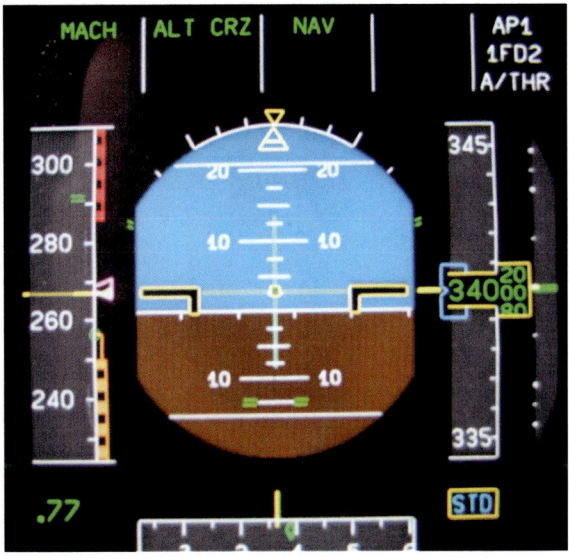

PFD

Present position, a route map and weather information are combined on another LCD, the Navigation Display (ND).

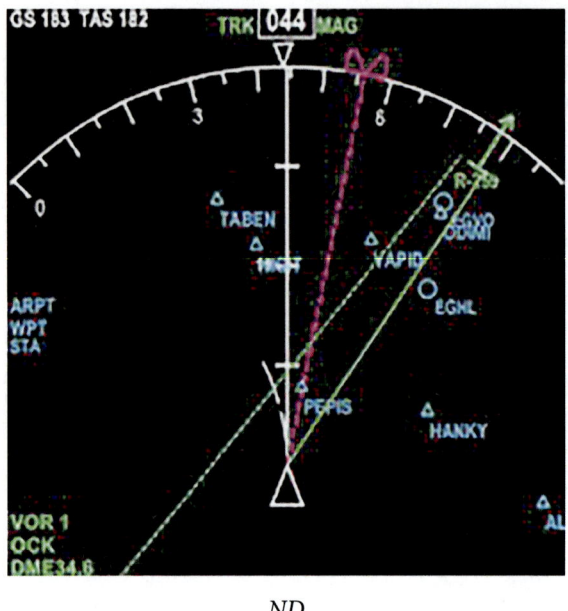

ND

The great thing about glass cockpits is it makes it much easier for pilots to know where they are, where they will be, and what the airplane is doing. This is good because it helps the pilot to FLY THE AIRPLANE.

One glance at the PFD and you can perform an instrument crosscheck - altitude, airspeed, heading, attitude, flight guidance mode, groundspeed, course, and track.

When you look at the ND you see the next waypoint, altitude restrictions, arrival times, nearest airports, winds, weather enroute, and even mountains (if you know how to adjust and interpret the radar). If you are thinking about changing your route, when the PM enters the proposed new route in the FMS the new route appears as a dotted line on the ND. You can immediately see if there is any conflicting weather along that route.

Engine and other aircraft system information are shown on other LCDs called System Displays.

SYSTEMS DISPLAYS

The latest Systems Displays (SD) show you a picture of an aircraft system (Electrical, Hydraulic, Pneumatic, Fuel, etc.) so that even a child could understand: For instance, select the electrical system display and you see a simple diagram of the airplane's electrical system - it shows the generators, transformers, electrical busses, and how they are all tied together.

Things that are working are green, things that are turned off are white, things with problems are yellow, and things that are broken are depicted in red. Using color in cockpit design philosophy is a deadly important aspect for aircraft manufacturers to consider. Even though English is the accepted international aviation language in all but a few countries, the philosophy of Green = Good, Yellow = Caution and Red = Bad is generally accepted worldwide.

This design philosophy becomes critical when you are training pilots who don't speak English as their first language. A box at the bottom of the screen lists what is turned off, what problems exist and what is broken. The pilot refers to a checklist to determine what to do if something has a problem or is broken.

Most new airplanes are equipped with automatic systems controllers that perform actions that pilots previously had to take - for instance, if #1 generator fails, a crosstie relay closes, and #2 generator automatically picks up the load. A yellow caution light illuminates to advise the pilot to look at the systems display). The systems display shows #1 generator yellow, the crosstie circuit changed from white to green, and a yellow message "GEN 1 FAIL" appears. The pilot looks up 'GEN 1 FAIL' in the checklist, and the checklist may tell the pilot something like "monitor electrical loads" or "Start Auxiliary Power Unit (APU) to provide backup electrical power".

In a typical "glass cockpit" airplane there is a selectable SD for each of the aircraft systems; Electrical, Fuel, Hydraulic, Pneumatic, Cabin Pressurization, etc. Each display clearly shows the status of every system component. The philosophy of Green = Good, Yellow = Caution and Red =Bad makes it easy for the pilot to quickly determine if systems are operating properly.

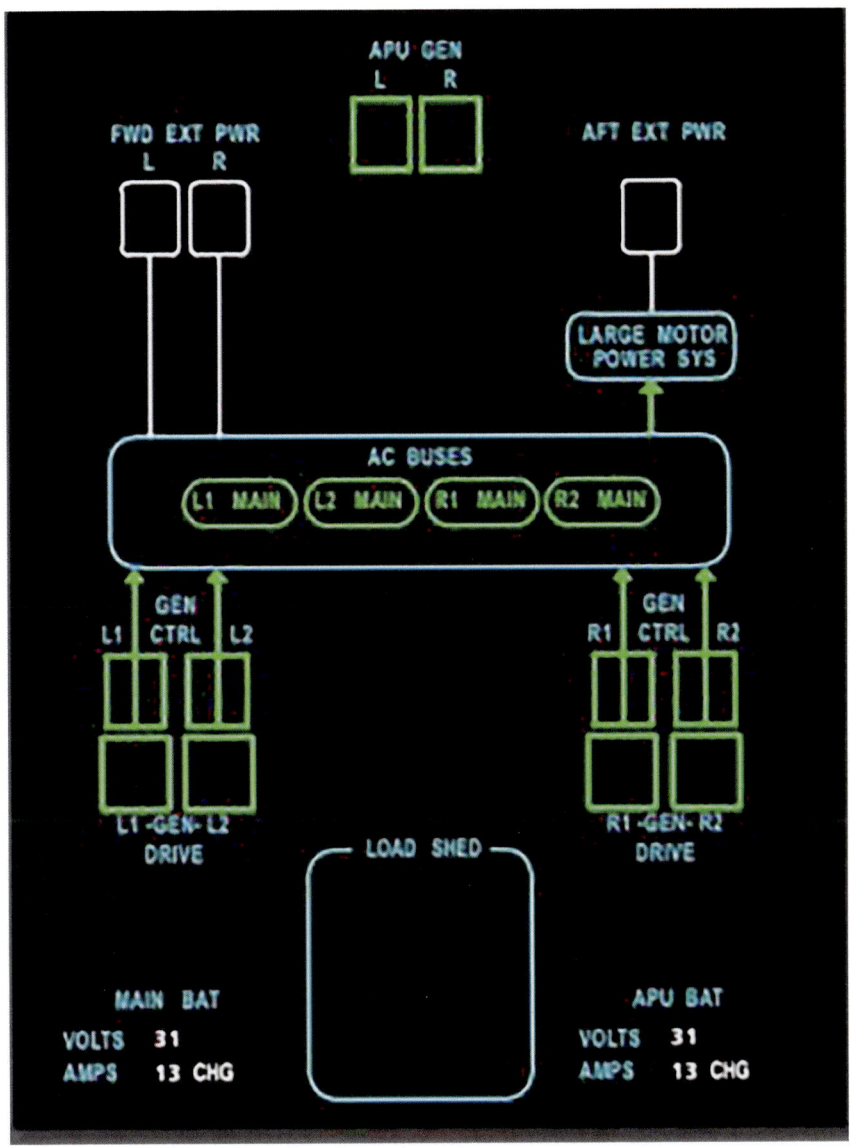

Typical Electrical System Display

The beauty in all this "Glass Cockpit" stuff is that if you use it wisely it gives the designated Pilot Flying (PF) much more time to do what a PF was designated to do: FLY THE AIRPLANE!

FLIGHT MANAGEMENT SYSTEMS (FMS)

Flight Management Systems (FMS) are one of the finest improvements in cockpit design that markedly improve a pilot's ability to FLY THE AIRPLANE.

FMS contain navigation and performance databases tailored to the individual airplane. Pilots enter flight plan information into the FMS Multi-Function Display Unit (MCDU), and the computer figures out if the airplane has enough fuel on board to do the job, optimum altitudes and speeds, and numerous other things the pilots need to know.

Typical FMS dual MCDU cockpit layout

The entire FMS flight plan route is displayed on the ND, and other important information (such as fuel remaining when you arrive at your destination) is displayed on the FMS MCDU. Once the airplane is in the air, the PF can engage the FMS to the autopilot and the FMS will FLY THE AIRPLANE along the flight plan route at the altitude selected by the pilot.

If there is a need to change the route due to weather or other reason, the PM inserts the new route into the MCDU. The proposed new route appears on the ND as a dashed line. The PM asks the PF to verify the proposed new route. The PF verifies that the dashed line is indeed correct, then orders PM to execute the proposed new route. The PM presses the Execute button and the line turns into a solid green line representing the new route. The FMS/autopilot will then fly along the new route. The pilots monitor what the FMS is doing and where they are by looking at the PFD, ND and MCDU.

It's easy to perform "what if" calculations enroute - for instance, if the weather at your destination is so bad that you are thinking you might have to divert to an alternate airport, the PM simply types in a secondary flight plan to your alternate airport, and the FMS figures out when you will arrive there and if you have enough fuel to do it. The proposed new route appears on the ND as a dotted line. All this time the FMS is navigating the airplane along the route you have been cleared to fly.

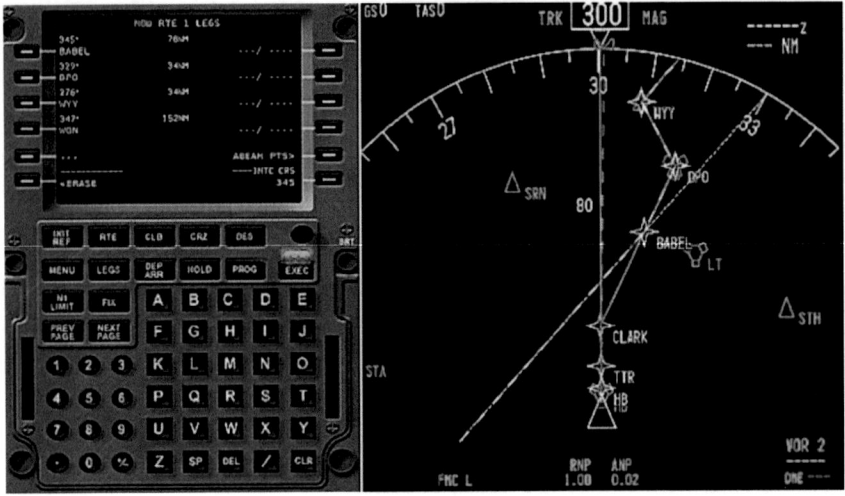

FMS route change "what if" prior to execution

COCKPIT WARNING SYSTEMS

Cockpit Warning Systems have constantly been improving over the years, but they can't keep you from doing something that will kill you - they can only warn. You still must FLY THE AIRPLANE.

GPWS TERRAIN warnings are still limited because you must be close to the terrain (And below 2500 feet) before they will tell you anything.

The latest Warning Systems will shout in your ear if it thinks you are about to hit something or land in the wrong configuration:

- If you take off and then start descending, you hear "DON'T SINK".

- If you go too near a mountain, it will tell you 'TERRAIN. TERRAIN"; if the terrain is rapidly rising it shouts 'WHOOP-WHOOP PULL UP! WHOOP-WHOOP, PULL UP!".

- Fly below the ILS glide slope and you will hear "GLIDE SLOPE, GLIDE SLOPE"!

- Forget to put the landing gear down, and as you descend below 500 feet you are told 'TOO LOW, GEAR! TOO LOW GEAR!".

- And if you forget to set landing flaps you will hear "TOO LOW, FLAPS, TOO LOW FLAPS" as you pass 300 feet.

Most airlines instruct their pilots to immediately start a climb any time they hear a GPWS warning. This is a good idea, because most GPWS alerts mean that you are probably not where you think you are.

So, what is the best thing to do? Right you are: FLY THE AIRPLANE!

TRAFFIC COLLISION WARNING SYSTEMS (TCAS)

Traffic Collision Avoidance Systems (TCAS) are now required on all new airliners being built.

They save lives!

Most people think "stealth" technology began with the F-117 and the B-2. That may be true if you are trying to see an airplane on radar, but if you are a pilot using your eyes to see and avoid other airplanes, there are literally thousands of "stealth" airplanes out there – they are called Cessnas, Pipers, Mooneys and hundreds of other small airplanes. They are almost impossible to see until you are right on top of them. TCAS can see these airplanes and tell you what to do to avoid hitting one.

Present versions of TCAS can only tell you what to do in the vertical plane, but versions under development will be capable of also telling you which way to turn to avoid a collision. Airplanes in your vicinity are displayed on the ND (Vertical Speed Indicator on non-glass cockpit airplanes). When an airplane gets near enough to you that you should be concerned, TCAS tells you 'TRAFFIC, TRAFFIC" and the threat airplane symbol in the ND changes from white to yellow. If the threat airplane is on a collision course, the symbol changes to red, and TCAS figures out what you should do. It will tell you to "CLIMB" or 'DESCEND" or "MONITOR VERTICAL SPEED" or one of several other suggestions. The vertical speed indicator on the PFD (or VSI) indicates in red the vertical speed range you should stay away from, and green the vertical speed you should fly to avoid the collision. But don't forget: You are not watching a TV show - you still must FLY THE AIRPLANE to avoid a midair collision!

You simply fly to the green vertical speed. When the threat of collision goes away, every indication goes back to normal and TCAS announces "CLEAR OF CONFLICT".

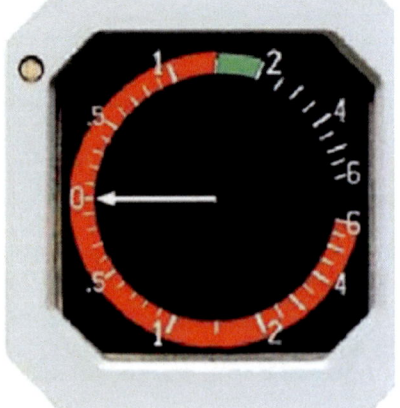

TCAS display on ND   *TCAS display on Vertical Speed Indicator*

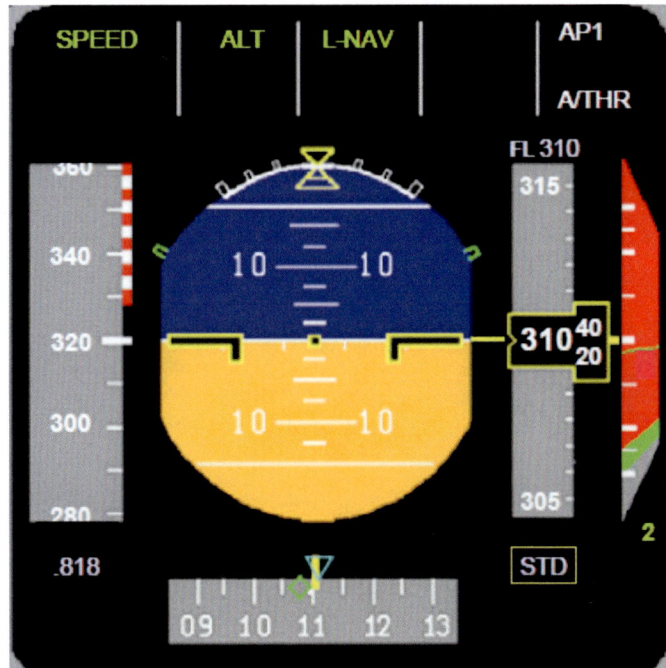

TCAS display on PFD

CHAPTER 5:

OOPS!

"OOPS" REDESIGNS OF THE PAST

As aircraft designers came up with new ways to make airplanes faster, fly higher, and carry stuff more efficiently, sometimes it takes an accident to alert designers that "Oops, when I changed that, I should have installed this gadget to tell the pilot he should do this". Here are a few examples:

- Someone came up with an idea to install retractable landing gear on an airplane. It was a great idea - it reduced drag, and the airplane could fly faster and farther. Then a few pilots forgot to FLY THE AIRPLANE and did a belly landing because they forgot to extend the landing gear. Oops, better install a warning when the engines are at low power (as in landing approach) and the landing gear is not down.

- High lift devices (wing flaps and slats) were installed on high-speed wings to allow for lower takeoff and landing speeds; Some pilot didn't complete the Before Takeoff Checklist (which calls for flaps to be set for takeoff), took off with the flaps up, and crashed. Oops, better install a takeoff warning to alert the pilot the flaps aren't properly set. While we're at it, let's also alert the pilot if the slats and trim tabs are not set or the parking brake is not off.

- One pilot who "didn't need a stupid checklist" left the pressurization outflow valve manually latched open, climbed to 25,000 feet, passed out from lack of oxygen, and crashed because nobody was FLYING THE AIRPLANE. Oops, better install a warning system that will let the pilot know when the cabin altitude goes above 10,000 feet. And also, oops, better talk about this incident in the training course to show pilots why they need a "stupid" checklist!

You might have noticed that in all three of the previous examples, aircraft design was changed because a pilot goofed. I used those examples for a reason - they show that nearly every time a design is changed, taking the pilot out of the information loop, an accident attributed to "pilot error" happens.

AN "OOPS" REDESIGN FOR THE FUTURE?

Dual FMS Controllers

When I was an airplane manufacturer's pilot assigned to train customer airline pilots how to FLY THIS NEW AIRPLANE, I have personally seen this picture hundreds of times training pilots who are using FMS for the first time. What is wrong with this picture?

What is wrong with this picture is that both pilots are preoccupied with doing something with this fascinating new gadget called FMS, and no one is FLYING THE AIRPLANE.

If I saw this happening during simulator training, I would freeze the simulator and ask, "Excuse me, but who is FLYING THE AIRPLANE"? That usually had the desired effect: From there on the PF started doing what PF means: FLY THE AIRPLANE.

After seeing this distraction occur so often it made me wonder if airplane manufacturers might want to consider designing a single FMS control unit that is accessible to either pilot. That way it makes it difficult for more than one pilot to operate the FMS Controller.

CHAPTER 6:
THE WRONG STUFF

In my opinion, one aircraft manufacturer decided to compensate for human frailties by designing the pilot out of the loop, creating contributing factors in at least two fatal accidents. Their airplanes were designed so that whatever crazy stunt the pilot tried, the computer would override the pilot's actions so that it is very difficult to exceed aircraft limitations. WHO IS THE PILOT FLYING – ME, OR THE FLIGHT COMPUTER PROGRAMMER?

Airbus once demonstrated their airplanes by showing off their "drunk pilot" routine: The demonstration pilot deliberately yanks the side stick controller from stop to stop, left and right, up, and down, then holds the controller in an extreme position. The airplane responds by gently banking or pitching to the normal limit, and not exceeding it unless the pilot applies extraordinary forces on the controller. The auto throttles and fly-by-wire flight controls will not allow the demonstration pilot to stall or over speed the airplane or overstress the airplane in any way.

These same features came back to bite the designers on Air France Flight 296Q – This was the first passenger flight of a new A-320. One of the plans for the flight was to fly two low passes at the Habsheim Air Show in Mulhouse France. The plan was to fly the first pass 100 feet above the runway at minimum speed, with gear down and flaps at approach setting. At the end of the runway, climb up to 1,000 feet, go out far enough to do a 180° turn, then perform a low pass on the opposite runway, then climb out and land at Basel-Mulhouse Airport All went well until the captain (PF) mistakenly descended below the planned 100 feet altitude - He momentarily became the Pilot NOT FLYING THE AIRPLANE:

When the airplane passed through 50 feet the auto flight system thought "We're landing," and went into the Flare mode which retarded the engines to flight idle. At the end of the runway the copilot pushed the TO/GA (Take Off/Go Around) button on the auto throttles as the captain raised the nose to climb. But the "Pilot Flying" (the auto flight system) decided the captain raised the nose too high and was risking a stall, ignored the captain's elevator command, and crashed into the trees off the end of the runway. The last two words heard on the Cockpit Voice Recorder (CVR) were the captain saying, "Aw S…!"

Three people died.

Air France Flight 296Q

One earlier version of this manufacturer's airplanes has a nasty habit of getting into a wild (and sometimes fatal) up and down oscillation if the pilot tries to manually override the autopilot. This usually happens when the pilot pushes the "go-around" button and then decides to land instead. When the auto throttle TOGA (Take Off Go Around) button is pushed, the engines advance to maximum thrust and the autopilot rapidly trims nose up. If the pilot then decides to land and pushes the nose down – the autopilot senses the nose going down and trims more nose up – if this battle continues the airplane will be trimmed full nose up, and if the pilot relaxes his forward pressure on the controls the airplane will zoom into a 60° - 75° climb until it stalls. The nose then falls until the airspeed builds up enough to zoom up again to another stall. This S-shaped wild ride continues until the pilot manages to get the airplane under control or the airplane crashes.

On U.S. manufactured airplanes, you push the TOGA button and then decide it is safe to do - you simply disconnect the autopilot and auto throttles, and land.

As a student of aviation safety, I have noticed a steady decline in the percentages of aircraft accidents over the last 30 years. It is safer to fly than it is to cross the street. Looking at the statistics, the percentage of accidents attributed to mechanical failure and weather has shown a steady decline, but the percentage of accidents caused by "pilot error" has been increasing. Why? Airplane technology has advanced as fast as scientific knowledge and design capabilities allow. Airplanes are very reliable and are getting better all the time.

But in my opinion Airbus has taken two very important safety features away from pilots: Tactile and visual feedback of throttle and flight control position.

A-320 Cockpit

MD-90 Cockpit

COCKPIT TACTILE AND VISUAL FEEDBACK

Airbus has made fantastic improvements in cockpit design, especially the installation of side-stick flight controls that give unobstructed view of the PFD and ND. However, this poses a situational awareness problem because the sidestick controllers are now just switches used to move the ailerons and elevators. The sidestick controllers are not linked to each other to give pilots visual and tactile feedback of commanded aileron and elevator position. Nor are the sidestick controllers linked to autopilot commanded aileron and elevator position.

Airbus throttle levers do not move in response to engine thrust settings but instead remain in detents set by the pilot: TO/GA, FLX/ MCT, CL, IDLE, REV and MAX. In U.S.-manufactured airliners the throttle levers always represent commanded thrust position either in manual or auto throttle operation. It is easy by either visual or tactile feedback to know where the thrust is set.

Space age technology is being incorporated into aircraft design as fast as it can be tested and certified. Fewer and fewer "oops" design changes are being required. On the other hand, there has been little if any change to "human design" in thousands of years. We get tired, distracted, and we are exceptionally poor monitors of automation. If we can't see, feel, or sense what the airplane is doing, we get confused. As more of the aircraft systems are automated, it becomes the design engineer's biggest challenge to keep the human pilot in the loop.

I sincerely believe these two design omissions contributed to the Air France Flight 447 crash. First, the PM had no tactile feedback in his sidestick controller that the PF was commanding full up elevator until shortly before crashing into the ocean. And second, it was impossible to visually determine from throttle lever position exactly where the thrust had been set.

U.S. MANUFACTURERS MAKE MISTAKES TOO

Every time an airplane manufacturer introduces a derivative version of an aircraft model, a major design consideration is airline customer demands to reduce crew training costs. For instance, all models of the Douglas DC-9, McDonnell Douglas MD-80/MD-90 and the Boeing 717 all have the same DC-9 FAA Type Rating. To transition from one model to the other only requires an abbreviated "Differences Training Course" as opposed to the lengthy "Type Rating Course".

Boeing was under the same pressure when introducing new models of the 737 family of airliners. They ran into a problem when they developed the new 737 Max series; for design reasons the new more powerful engines had to be moved forward, which introduced different pitch handling characteristics when engine power settings were changed. These characteristics were so different from other 737 models that there was a concern that extensive flight crew training would be required, discouraging airlines from buying the 737 Max.

So, Boeing design engineers came up with a gadget called the Maneuvering Characteristics Augmentation System (MCAS), which was intended to automatically mimic flight behavior of the previous generation of 737s. For some reason they didn't include in the design redundant backup failure modes (they only used one Angle Of Attack {AOA} sensor in the design). For another unknown reason they decided not to describe MCAS or provide failure mode Abnormal Procedures the Flight Crew Operating Manual (FCOM). Airline flight crews were not told or trained about MCAS. And to top it all off, the FAA approved the 737 Max entering service in 2017 knowing that airline pilots were not aware that MCAS even existed! The result:

October 29, 2018: B-737 Max Lion Air Flight 610 single AOA malfunction causes MCAS to trim aircraft pitch into a situation crew was not trained to handle. The airplane crashed into Java Sea, 189 fatalities.

Lion Air Flight 610

March 10, 2019: B-737 Max Ethiopian Airlines Flight 302 Single AOA malfunction causes MCAS to trim aircraft pitch into a situation crew was not trained to handle. The airplane crashed into a farm field, 157 fatalities.

Ethiopian Airlines Flight 302

The point I am trying to make here is that technology has not yet made it to the level that the pilot can be safely taken out of the loop. No manufacturer has yet been able to come up with a computer that cares whether it crashes or not. The human pilot is still the best safety insurance we have. Aircraft designers and manufacturers must realize this fact, and carefully consider the human factors aspects when they build airplanes.

To quote the comedian Rich Cook: "Programming today is a race between software engineers striving to build bigger and better idiot-proof programs, and the universe trying to produce bigger and better idiots.

So far, the universe is winning."

CHAPTER 7:

FLY THE AIRPLANE

Over the years, there have been an alarming number of aircraft accidents caused by pilots failing to do one of the first things you are taught to do in pilot training: FLY THE AIRPLANE!!!

MY EARLY EXPERIENCE

FLY THE AIRPLANE was drummed into my brain by my C-124 guru Captain Thomas C. Hammond, a WWII veteran and legendary pilot that would take writing another book to describe his exploits. Let's just say that Tom was a great teacher, and I applied his FLY THE AIRPLANE discipline soon after I became a C-124 Aircraft Commander.

One of the most important things Tom Hammond taught me about flying is that no matter what happens: A pilot must always be there to FLY THE AIRPLANE, even if the autopilot is engaged. Autopilots are not pilots. The C-124 autopilot had a nasty habit of sometimes putting the airplane into a descent then disconnecting.

One night after a long day we were on a 6-hour flight from Vietnam to Japan. When we got to cruise altitude, I told my copilot I was going to rest my eyes for about an hour in the crew bunk (There were 3 crew bunks in the rear of the flight deck). About 30 minutes later in my bunk, I saw the bathroom light come on when the door was opened. I could have sworn that it was the copilot going into the bathroom. I looked forward and saw an empty cockpit. It WAS the copilot! The bathroom door had a hasp with a combination lock; we secured valuables there on overnight stays. I put the lock on the door, then went up and strapped myself in the pilot's seat. I then turned the autopilot off and made several abrupt nose-down, nose-up and bank maneuvers. I could hear the copilot screaming trying to get out of the locked bathroom. I let him stay in there for about 45 minutes to teach him a lesson. Then I told the navigator to let him out.

I don't think he ever allowed another empty cockpit for the rest of his flying career!

Lesson learned.

MY SPANISH "FLY THE AIRPLANE" CHALLENGE

In 1968 I was transferred to Torrejon Air Base, Spain as a Controller in Military Airlift Command's Europe-Africa Area Command Post. Since I had a "desk" job at Torrejon, I had to get my minimum of 4 hours pilot time each month so I could get my flight pay. I was assigned to fly the C-54 Skymaster, the military version of the DC-4.

The training program was a joke: They never even provided me with a flight manual to study; they just put me in the left seat, and we went flying. So, I ordered the instructor to complete the appropriate checklists, and I FLEW THE AIRPLANE. When the instructor retarded a throttle to idle and said, "simulated engine failure #4 engine", I said "I have no idea what the Engine Failure Checklist tells me to do, so I'll FLY THE AIRPLANE, and you accomplish the checklist. After a four-hour flight with multiple approaches, landings and simulated emergencies, the instructor said, "You are now qualified as an Aircraft Commander in the C-54".

C-54 Skymaster

With such a terrible training program (no Flight Manuals, hasty qualification flights, etc.), I often wondered why this C-54 Squadron had such a perfect safety record. Then I looked at the pilots who were allowed to fly these airplanes. They all knew how to FLY THE AIRPLANE!

One of these people was Colonel Gail Halvorsen, a veteran C-54 pilot who was known as "The Candy Bomber of the Berlin Airlift". Colonel Halvorsen was the smoothest pilot I have ever flown with. It was an honor to meet and fly with this legend and watch him FLY THE AIRPLANE.

Candy Bomber Colonel Gail Halvorsen 100th birthday October 10, 2020

Not having a C-54 Flight Manual came back to bite me one time. I was flying at 10,000 feet when I encountered icing conditions. I did what I had done hundreds of times before in the C-124 – I turned on the wing deicer system. A few minutes later it seemed that the wings were icing up anyway – I had the engines at full power and was losing altitude. I advised Air Traffic Control of my problem, and they cleared me to descend. I finally was able to level off at 6,000 feet, where the air temperature was above freezing, and the ice melted.

I later discovered that the C-54 has inflatable deicer boots to de-ice the wings

(Unlike the C-124, which uses hot air in the wing leading edges to melt the ice). In the C-54, you must FIRST let ice buildup on the wing leading edge BEFORE you inflate the boot to break the ice off. I had let ice buildup on the inflated boot, creating so much drag that I couldn't maintain altitude. If I had been in mountainous terrain,

THAT could have turned into another Controlled Flight Into Terrain (CFIT) accident.

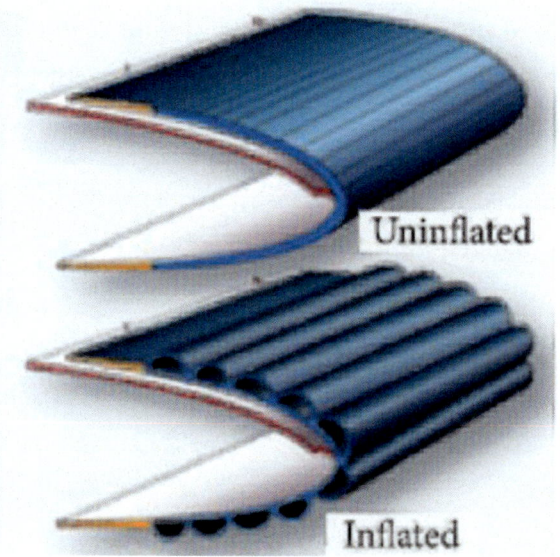

Pneumatic Deicer Boot

I feel I get a little help from Higher Headquarters occasionally!

TRAIN TO FLY THE AIRPLANE

As noted in Chapter Three, most modern training programs require that one crew member be designated as Pilot Flying (PF), and the other be designated as Pilot Monitoring (PM). Generally, this means that the PF is responsible for manually flying the airplane or operating the autopilot and auto throttles, and the PM is responsible for monitoring the PF's performance while also accomplishing other duties (check-lists, flap/slat/landing gear operation, radio, monitoring deviations in airspeed, altitude, or course, and adjusting the Flight Management System (FMS) allowing the PF to view the changes prior to execution).

I have personally observed many deviations to the PF/PM concept in training scenarios. For instance, I have seen pilots transitioning to a glass cockpit/FMS airplane get overwhelmed with the high technology and forget about basic flying. Many times, in the flight simulator, I would see both pilots with their heads down, playing with the FMS. I would freeze the simulator and ask: "Who is FLYING the airplane?". The blank expressions on their faces reminded me of a hog looking at a wristwatch!

This is the most critical issue to impart to pilots during initial and recurrent training: no matter what happens, the PF must FLY THE AIRPLANE!!!

CHAPTER 8:

THREE ACCIDENTS

AIR FRANCE A-330

Air France Flight 447 was at cruise altitude enroute from Brazil to Paris. The captain went to the rest compartment, and two copilots were in the captains and copilots' seats. The copilot was designated PF. They encountered icing in a thunderstorm, which rendered the airspeed indicators inoperative (not supposed to happen). Because of the airspeed malfunction, the auto flight system falsely sensed and annunciated an overspeed condition. The auto flight system disconnected the auto throttles and autopilot. The PF applied back pressure to the sidestick controller. The aircraft went into a climb until it went into a full stall (which resulted in a visual and aural stall warning) and stayed in a full stall until the aircraft crashed in the Atlantic Ocean.

There were no survivors.

After the digital flight and voice recorders had been recovered and examined, the accident investigation team discovered that the right (copilot's) sidestick controller was in the full aft position the entire time from the overspeed warning until just before impact with the water.

NOBODY WAS FLYING THE AIRPLANE!! It would have been so easy to prevent this accident if the PF had followed my FLY THE AIRPLANE line of thought. Let me explain:

PROBLEM:

Icing in airspeed sensing system causes false OVERSPEED warning.

THIS IS NOT SUPPOSED TO HAPPEN because design redundancy prevents it. Confused flight computers order the autopilot and auto throttles to disconnect.

SOLUTION: PF MUST:

FLY THE AIRPLANE: Check instruments – airspeed high, level flight attitude, engines indicate at cruise setting.

FLY THE AIRPLANE: reduce power, raise nose until airspeed returns to normal. Airspeed indication still high with aural OVERSPEED warning, STALL warning sounds.

FLY THE AIRPLANE: Check instruments – airspeed high, nose high attitude, engines indicate idle.

FLY THE AIRPLANE: Think - "I have two conflicting warnings – OVERSPEED and STALL. Nose down and high engine power will make me overspeed, but my nose is high, and my engines indicate idle."

FLY THE AIRPLANE: Think – "High nose and low power make the airplane stall. The overspeed warning must be false."

FLY THE AIRPLANE: Lower the nose, add power, and ignore the false overspeed warning.

FLY THE AIRPLANE: After the stall warning silences, let airplane accelerate until a cruise power setting results in a normal aircraft pitch attitude.

FLY THE AIRPLANE: If false overspeed warning persists, nuisance warning may be silenced by opening the appropriate circuit breaker.

FLY THE AIRPLANE: Approach and landing with inoperative airspeed indication can be accomplished using appropriate power settings that give normal pitch attitude or angle of attack (if AOA indicator is installed).

This accident could have prevented if the Pilot Flying had only FLOWN THE AIRPLANE.

Air France Flight 447

AIR CANADA B-767

Air Canada Flight 143 was dispatched to fly with a faulty Fuel Quantity Indicating System (FQIS). To do this, the 767 Minimum Equipment List (MEL) requires that prior to each flight the actual fuel quantity in each fuel tank be visually checked with a dipstick, and the quantity readings be given to the captain. The dipstick quantity readings are marked as pounds of fuel. Flight 143 Captain Pearson mistakenly entered kilograms (instead of pounds) of fuel into the Flight

Management System (FMS) computer. The FMS indicated adequate fuel on board for the flight from Montreal to Edmonton. Because of this mistake the actual onboard was only 45% of what was required for the flight. Guess what happened? About halfway through the flight, the airplane ran out of fuel and both engines flamed out. Flight 473 then became the largest and heaviest glider in the world.

Fortunately, Captain Pearson was an experienced glider pilot, so he was familiar with flying techniques almost never used in commercial flight. First Officer Quintal searched for a Two Engine Flameout Checklist, but there was none. The reason there was no checklist is because an all-engine flameout is not supposed to happen; All airliner manufacturers must prove to the FAA that the chances of this happening are greater than "ten to the minus ninth" (Less than once in a billion flights) before the airplane can be certified.

As you can imagine, the 767 isn't a very efficient glider – it has a glide ratio of about 12:1 (travels 12 feet forward for every 1 foot of altitude). Modern sailplanes can have glide ratios up to above 50:1. Because Flight 143 had about the same glide ratio as a brick, no suitable airports were within gliding range. First Officer Quintal proposed landing at the former RCAF Air Base Gimli a closed air force base where he had once served as a pilot for the Royal Canadian Air Force. It was the only long runway within gliding distance. What they didn't know was that the Gimli runway was now being used as a dragstrip.

As they approached the Gimli runway Captain Pearson realized he was too high. He used the Emergency Landing Gear Extension procedure (using gravity to lower the landing gear and lock it into place). The main gear locked into position, but the nose wheel did not.

He was still too high, but a 360° turn would put them too low. So, Pearson decided to execute a side-slip maneuver to increase drag and reduce altitude. This, performed by applying rudder in one direction and ailerons in the other direction (this maneuver is commonly used in gliders and light aircraft to increase the descent rate without increasing forward speed). I have never seen it used on a large airplane like a 767; but Pearson was a glider pilot, and he knew how to FLY THE AIRPLANE.

To make things even more interesting, when he was a few miles out Pearson noticed that a drag race was taking place on the far end of the runway. Just before touchdown he barely missed hitting two boys on bicycles.

After touchdown Pearson applied heavy breaking to stop before he reached the dragstrip. The nose landing gear collapsed, adding drag to shorten the stopping distance.

There were no serious injuries.

Captain Pearson FLEW THE AIRPLANE.

The Gimli Glider

U.S. AIRWAYS A-320

U.S. Airways Flight 1549 departed New York's LaGuardia Airport enroute to Charlotte, North Carolina.

About three minutes after takeoff, the airplane flew into a flock of Canadian geese. Birds flew into both engines, causing them to lose power, turning flight 1549 into a 155-seat glider. Captain Sullenberger immediately realized he was too far from any airport to land, so he did the only thing he could – he ditched the airplane in the Hudson River.

There were *no* fatalities. Captain Sullenberger FLEW THE AIRPLANE!!

US Airways Flight 1549

All the accidents I described above were situations that are not covered in airline training programs, because they weren't supposed to happen. But they did.

CHAPTER 9:

FLY THE SAILPLANE

I believe the best way for anyone to learn what it means to FLY THE AIRPLANE is to start their training in gliders/sailplanes.

The reason I say this is simple: A basic glider/sailplane has nothing to distract you from FLYING THE AIRPLANE; no engine, no radio, electrical, avionics, transponder, hydraulic system. The only flight instruments you have are airspeed, altimeter, and variometer (rate of climb/descent indicator).

And you don't really need any flight instruments if you believe this pilot. In 1958 during the last part of my USAF pilot training at Greenville AFB Mississippi, there was a local crop duster pilot who would take us up for a thrill ride in his Stearman crop duster biplane. I had one ride with the old guy. Once I was strapped in the front seat, he had me put on a leather helmet with earphones equipped with tubes connected to a funnel in the rear cockpit. This was the one-way interphone: The old guy would shout instructions to me in the funnel, and if I understood I would nod and do what he had shouted. There were no throttle lever or instruments (airspeed, altimeter, compass, rate of climb, engine instruments) at all in the front cockpit, but there was a control stick and rudder pedals. The old guy said that he would take care of the throttle and I could "FLY THE AIRPLANE".

Before he got in the back seat and started the engine, I asked him "How can I tell my airspeed if I don't have an airspeed indicator", and he replied, "Listen to the struts" (The metal extrusions holding the upper and lower wings together. The sound they make changes pitch as airspeed changes). Funny enough, if you are not completely tone deaf, it *works*!

He shouted, "You make the takeoff and head for that tree at the end of the grass strip". I did, but when I thought it was time to climb the old guy wouldn't let me pull the stick back. He kept holding forward pressure on the stick until we were about 50 feet from the tree, then he released the pressure, the stick came back into my lap and the airplane went straight up! I became a crop duster! It was an exciting 15-minute ride - he let me "use" the flight controls, but the old guy was FLYING THE AIRPLANE all the time.

I can truthfully say that I have been able to fly an airplane simply by only using three of my five senses: Sight, Sound and Touch. I'm not too sure about the other two senses – Smell and Taste (maybe even Smell if you – Oh, never mind!).

Stearman

This even works on big airplanes: I know, a Boeing or Airbus airliner, a C-17 or F-35 doesn't have struts you can listen to, but you can still use most of your five senses to get a feel of what is happening, enabling you to FLY THE AIRPLANE.

But back to gliders, in the beginning of WWII, some of the best aviators were German Luftwaffe fighter pilots who had initially been trained in gliders when they were teenagers. Because they knew how to FLY THE AIRPLANE, this ability many times enabled them to save their combat-damaged fighter plane.

Toward the end of the war the Japanese military, in a last-ditch effort to defeat the U.S. Navy, resorted to using Kamikaze airplanes to attack U.S. Navy ships (Kamikaze means Divine Wind, a reference to the typhoon that destroyed Kublai Khan's entire fleet of ships as they were trying to invade Japan in 1274).

There were few experienced pilots left at that stage of the war, so they resorted to using gliders to train young men with no experience. The only thing they learned was how to FLY THE AIRPLANE into a U.S. Navy ship, the bigger the better.

For a young Japanese man at that time, becoming a Kamikaze Pilot was *not* some lunatic act of desperation, but the ultimate act of patriotism of a Samurai warrior.

MY HIGH FLIGHT EXPERIENCE

In the U.S. Air Force Aviation Cadets program, many students were ordered by their instructors to memorize the following poem called HIGH FLIGHT, written by John Gillespie Magee Jr., a WWII Anglo American Royal Canadian Air Force fighter pilot:

HIGH FLIGHT

Oh! I have slipped the surly bonds of Earth,

And danced the skies on laughter-silvered wings;

Sunward I've climbed, and joined the tumbling

Mirth of sun-split clouds-

and done a hundred things you have not dreamed of –

wheeled and soared and swung High in the sunlit silence.

Hov'ring there, I've chased the shouting wind along

and flung my eager craft through footless halls of air.

Up, up the long delirious burning blue

I've topped the wind-swept heights with easy grace,

where never lark, or single eagle flew;

and, while with silent, lifting mind I've trod

the high untrespassed sanctity of space,

put out my hand and touched the face of God.

All pilots get to experience transcending the earth and are exposed to the elements of this poem such as aerobatics and having fun maneuvering around and over cumulus clouds, but as far as "Putting out my hand, and touching the face of God" most pilots rarely experience that. But I did.

In1966 I was stationed at Robins AFB, GA. I added a Commercial Glider rating to my pilot license. At a nearby glider training school, I got qualified in the Schweizer 2-22 glider, then the Schweizer 2-34 and 1-26 sailplanes. The difference between a glider and a sailplane is that a sailplane has a better glide ratio.

In 1969 I was stationed in Germany. I joined a German glider club based at a small airfield near Mainz. I flew the Schleicher KA7 2-seat and the KA8 single seat sailplanes. We only did winch launches to about 900 feet and were restricted to fly below 1900 feet within a few miles' radius from the airfield. It was fun though, and I learned a lot about how different it is to fly a sailplane as opposed to flying a regular airplane.

For instance - flying a regular airplane, especially when flying on instruments, the pilot makes thousands of fine adjustments of the flight controls to keep the airplane precisely on course. In a sailplane you don't have an engine to keep you in the air; you only have ALTITUDE, AIR SPEED, LIFT, and BRAINS.

At first, I couldn't understand how the other guys were staying aloft for over an hour after a winch launch to 900 feet and I could only stay up about 30 to 45 minutes, I asked an instructor to go up with me to see what I was doing wrong.

I was INSTRUMENT FLYING! I was making thousands of small flight control corrections, not realizing that in a sailplane every time you move the flight controls you lose some LIFT - for the best lift/drag ratio you need to move the flight controls as little as possible.

My High Flight "putting out my hand and touching the face of God" experience occurred on the northwestern side of Hawaii's Oahu Island around 1974: Dillingham Airfield, on the North Shore area of Oahu, offers glider rental to "ridge soar" the cliffs of the North Shore.

Ridge soaring is this: The North Shore normally has a constant ocean breeze of 15-20 mph coming from the North. When the breeze hits the cliffs, it has nowhere to go but up. If you fly a glider or sailplane parallel to the cliffs in this updraft you can climb from your 1000-foot release altitude from the towplane to 2000-2500 in the updraft lift, or even higher depending on the wind speed.

Ridge soaring North Shore cliffs

That day I rented a Schweizer 2-22 glider. It is called a glider because of its low glide ratio of 22/1 (it sinks 1 foot for every 22 feet of travel. Sailplanes haver higher glide ratios, some over 55/1). The 2-22 had no radio or ATC Transponder, and the only instruments were airspeed and altimeter.

During the preflight briefing I was told where I should fly to take advantage of the best lift, and to keep an eye out for their white pickup truck. If I saw the truck parked perpendicular on the runway, that was the emergency signal to immediately return to the airfield and land.

I did an aerotow launch and the airplane towed me to 1000 feet near the ridge where I released the tow cable. I flew back and forth parallel to the ridge and soon climbed to around 2000 feet in the ridge lift. For around 45 minutes I was having a ball going back and forth enjoying the beautiful view when I noticed the truck parked perpendicular on the runway.

I immediately headed back toward the airfield and started to descend. I looked to the left and saw why they wanted me to land - a thunderstorm was rapidly coming in from the north (later they told me that this happens nearly every afternoon around the same time).

The thunderstorm was pushing the air in front of it around 50-60 mph and this greatly increased the ridge lift. I suddenly found myself at 4000 feet and climbing! I extended full air brakes and increased the airspeed to the redline speed of 98mph, but I was still climbing! I had enough altitude to fly over the mountains and land at Honolulu International Airport or Naval Air Station Barbers Point, but if I did that that it would cost me my pilots license and a heavy fine for entering controlled airspace without a radio or transponder. What to do?

At that point I feel that God put out His hand and touched my arms and legs and showed me what I needed to do - slow down to just above stall speed, then put the glider into a full side slip with the air brakes fully extended —I hadn't done a side slip maneuver since 1958 in the early stages of my USAF pilot training!

Side Slip

To do the side slip maneuver I rolled the aircraft to a 90-degree bank and used full rudder to make the fuselage face straight down. This gave me the highest drag and sink rate possible. Then I extended the airbrakes, creating so much more drag that the glider fell like a brick!

I finally landed the glider and stopped on the runway just as the rain started pouring down. I stayed in the cockpit with the air brake extended while the guys in the white pickup truck got thoroughly soaked putting sandbags on the wings to keep the glider from being blown away

This whole episode reminds me of two Bible verses attributed to King Solomon, written sometime around 970-930 BCE:

Trust in the Lord with all your heart.

And do not depend on your own understanding.

If you Seek His will in all you do,

He will show you which path to take.

(Proverbs 3:5,6)

I think if King Solomon were observing this incident today, He would have modified the last verse to say: Seek His will in all you do, He will show you how to FLY THE AIRPLANE, whatever an "airplane" is.

"Whatever an *Airplane* is, you should FLY IT!": *King Solomon, 2022*

CHAPTER 10:

CONTROLLED FLIGHT INTO TERRAIN

AIRPLANES SHOULDN'T CRASH INTO THINGS

Weird accidents have been happening since the early days of aviation: airplanes with no malfunctions flying under perfect control run into things they shouldn't - mountains, swamps, the Empire State Building, radio towers, etc. These kinds of accidents happened so frequently that someone decided they should have a name. They are now called Controlled Flight Into Terrain (CFIT).

My interest in CFIT accidents began when I was a 23-year-old C-124 pilot in Tachikawa Air Base, Japan. I will never forget that night.

CFIT ACCIDENT #1 – THIS COULD HAVE BEEN ME!

On May 24th, 1962, I was on a four-hour night training flight out of Tachikawa. The weather was very poor, with heavy rain and low visibility. We departed Tachikawa but did all the training at Yokota Air Base because they had a long runway and two precision approaches

- GCA and ILS. We practiced both types of approaches. Each student got two approaches with touch-and-go landings and one with a full stop landing. Then the next student would strap into the pilot's seat and repeat the drill. The last student would make the full stop landing at Tachikawa.

After we finished our training flight, we landed at Tachikawa and did an engine-running crew change. The other crew had an instructor pilot and six students from my squadron. We all knew each other. Less than two hours after they departed, I heard that the airplane had crashed into a mountain near Yokota Air Base, killing all on board. I was shocked.

But for the grace of God, I could have been scheduled to be on THAT training flight instead of the one before it!

CFIT Accident #1. Mount Chichibu, Japan 1962

CFIT ACCIDENT #2

In 1966, to avoid thunderstorms, a C-124 flew off course in Spain and crashed into a mountain, killing all on board. There was no Air

Traffic Control Radar to warn them they were heading toward high terrain. I had flown with this pilot in 1963 when we were stationed together at Tachikawa.

The two C-124 CFIT crashes happened on airplanes with limited instrumentation to provide the pilot with situational awareness: navigation radios with an indicator that pointed in the direction of a navigation radio station (or a thunderstorm in the case of the Automatic Direction Finder {ADF} navigation radio) ; primitive weather radar that made it difficult to discriminate between a mountain and a cloud; and nothing in the cockpit to show the pilots exactly where they were relative to obstacles or terrain.

These two accidents were correctly attributed to Pilot Error. But the real cause was "Lack of Information to Show Pilots Where They Were Relative to Terrain". I guess it was easier for Accident Investigators to list the accident cause as the abbreviation "PE" instead of "LOITSPWTWRTT".

All I could find of C-124 CFIT Crash in Spain

CFIT ACCIDENT #3

My first training assignment at Douglas Aircraft Company after retiring from the Air Force was to instruct a crew from an Eastern European airline on the MD-80. They performed well during their training at Long Beach, but in 1981 I learned they were both killed during an approach to an airport in Corsica, when they turned the wrong way and crashed into a mountain.

Inex Adria Flight 1308

CFIT ACCIDENT #4
LED TO MY INVENTION

While I was working at McDonnell Douglas, an American Airlines Boeing 757 crashed into a mountain near Cali, Colombia. I couldn't believe that this could happen to a state-of-the-art airplane! This was the FOURTH CFIT accident that personally affected me. All four accidents were attributed to "Pilot Error". The two C-124 accidents had contributing factors of having rather primitive navigation equipment, but the MD-80 had a Ground Proximity Warning System (GPWS) and the B-757 had both GPWS and Global Positioning System (GPS).

I decided to see if I could figure out how to prevent CFIT accidents. I researched Controlled Flight Into Terrain extensively. I concluded that the *only* reason airplanes run into terrain or man-made obstacles is that the pilots didn't know exactly where they were going — otherwise known as "Lack of Situational Awareness"!

I designed a GPS based gadget that did what no other terrain avoidance system in existence did. While all state-of-the-art terrain avoidance systems use a terrain data base and GPS to calculate predicted flight path and generate a terrain warning, my gadget goes one step further - When my gadget predicts an impending collision, the pilot is alerted to look at the display screen: it shows a color 3D "look- out-the-window-on-a-clear-day" view of the terrain/obstacles. The predicted flight path is displayed as a "finger" pointing from the airplane to where the airplane is predicted to be. When the finger touches an obstacle, the fingertip turns red. The terrain/obstacle is displayed in 3D color; To avoid hitting the obstacle, the pilot simply maneuvers the airplane to move the flight path "finger" over or away from the collision point (over if aircraft performance permits, or away the obstacle until clear of it). When clear of the collision risk the finger turns green.

McDonnell Douglas (now Boeing) paid for the patent (US Patent # 6,021,374) and owned the licensing rights to it until they stopped paying the annual fee to the U.S. Patent Office. Because of that the patent has expired. Anyone who wants to build my gadget can use the information in the patent without having to pay royalties to Boeing.

I still think my gadget is a good idea. Anybody want to build a prototype?

CHAPTER 11:

I FLEW THE MD-90

I have never been more deeply involved in any airplane than I was with the MD-90, the biggest and best member of the DC-9 family.

WRITING THE FLIGHT MANUALS

During the design and initial production phase, fellow pilot Frank Anderson and I were tasked to write the MD-90 Flight Crew Operating Manual (FCOM), 3-volumes consisting of Systems Description, Performance and Operating Procedures. To write this book, we had to learn about every part of the airplane; how all systems worked, what were the operating limitations, what are the normal operating procedures, what to do if something broke, how do you FLY THE AIRPLANE, everything a flight crew needed to know to operate a MD-90.

I worked closely with our MD-90 launch customer Delta Airlines to make sure their FCOM was FAA certified prior to their first revenue flight. I also was the Lead Pilot on the Japan Air System MD-90 program and participated in translating their FCOM into Japanese.

When the MD-90 entered the Flight Test program, Chief MD-90 Test Pilot Bill Jones allowed me to participate starting with the second flight of the airplane. As I learned all about the MD-90 I ended up writing the MD-90 Production Flight Procedures Manual (PFPM), the checklist used to prepare a newly assembled airplane for its customer acceptance flight.

PRODUCTION FLIGHT TEST

In a Production Test, the entire airplane, freshly off the assembly line, is completely tested to make sure everything works as advertised:

A complete ground inspection, to include testing, is performed to make sure that no loose nuts and bolts are there to cause trouble. Flight controls are maneuvered to confirm that they move properly, all systems (electrical, hydraulic, pneumatic, flight instruments, radios, nosewheel steering, thrust reversers and brakes) are checked to ensure they are functioning normally, ending with a high-speed rejected takeoff with maximum braking.

During the Production Test Flight every bit of the airplane is taken to its limits to make sure all systems are functioning as designed: such as stall warning, overspeed warning, cabin depressurization to ensure that the cockpit cabin altitude alert sounds and indicates at 10,000 cabin altitude, oxygen masks automatically deploy at 12,000 feet cabin altitude. Verify inflight engine shutdown and restart, autopilot and avionics operation, including autopilot approaches and autoland are successful.

Japan Air System Production Flight Test MD-90, June 1995

After you have flown a few Production Test Flights, you get a good working knowledge of how to FLY THE AIRPLANE! You have taken the airplane to its extreme limits, and you get an almost "listen to the struts" feel for how the airplane is performing (If you remember what the old crop duster pilot told be about how to judge the speed of a Stearman biplane).

AIR SHOWS AND MARKETING TOURS

I was fortunate to be a pilot with the 1993 Paris Airshow and Tour team. Besides participating in the Paris Air Show we conducted marketing flights in Italy, England, and Sweden.

1993 Paris Airshow and Tour crew

My most enjoyable flight on this tour was in Stockholm. Japan Air System Captain Tanaka flew the airplane, and I was the copilot. Our passengers were mostly Scandinavian Airline (SAS) employees. I made the P.A. announcements in both English and Japanese. After Captain Tanaka made a perfect landing on a wet runway, I thanked the passengers for flying Japan Air System.

I was a pilot on the MD-90 Asia tour when we took a Delta MD-90 to Japan, Korea, and China.

Delta MD-90

My highlight of this tour was the flight I flew out of Beijing. The passengers were mostly pilots from a Chinese airline who were also military fighter pilots. The CEO of McDonnell Douglas was also on board, and he asked me to show these "fighter pilots" how well the MD-90 can perform. The Delta MD-90 V-2500 engines have a maximum thrust selectable to either 25,000 or 28,000 pounds. We were carrying minimum fuel and were very light weight, so I selected 28,000 thrust and climbed out at V2 (Minimum engine-out) speed. The climb out pitch attitude was about 45°. The fighter pilots were impressed.

MY TRIBUTE TO BOB HOOVER

I have always admired Bob Hoover (1922-2016) as being the best pilot ever when it comes to FLYING THE AIRPLANE. He just had that natural talent for making the impossible look easy. I wish I could execute the amazing maneuver he did in an Aero Commander: performing a perfect one-handed 1g barrel roll, using the other hand to pour iced tea from a pitcher into a glass without spilling a drop. My problem is that I have never been able to do anything near a perfect barrel roll.

But his energy management finale intrigued me. Every bit of the routine made sense to me: If you accumulate enough extra energy (in this case speed) you can extract maximum performance from the airplane even if you are short of the other forms of energy (altitude and thrust).

I spent hundreds of hours in the MD-90 Engineering Simulator developing procedures to include in the MD-90 Flight Crew Operating Manual (FCOM): Normal operating procedures as well as abnormal/emergency procedures such as Engine Failure, Aborted Takeoff, Stall Recovery, Rapid Decompression and Emergency Descent.

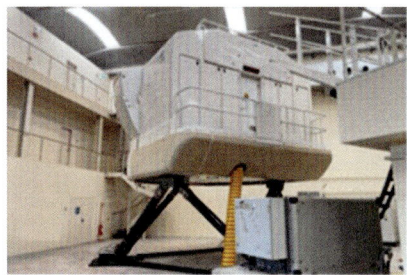 

MD-90 Engineering Simulator

While I was perfecting these procedures, I was taking the MD-90 to the ultimate extremes of its performance capabilities. Late one night after testing the Ground Proximity Warning System (GPWS) aural warning (TOO LOW GEAR, TOO LOW FLAPS, PULL UP and TERRAIN) functions, I thought "That last low pass at LAX looked like the opening of a Bob Hoover's Energy Management Finale!" Hmm!

The GPWS tests were complete for the night, I was alone in the flight simulator and the next crew wasn't scheduled to come in for six hours. So, I decided to try my own "Charlie Wood Energy Management Finale" at Los Angeles International Airport (LAX).

Our MD-90 Engineering Simulator was equipped with realistic visual scenarios for several airports, including LAX. It even had a realistic parking scene at Terminal D, Gate D-10. I planned out the following scenario:

- Configuration: Autopilot/auto throttles - Off. Flaps, slats, landing gear -Retracted, Auxiliary Power Unit (APU) – On, to provide electric power and alternate electric hydraulic pump pressure.

- Start: 5 miles from runway 24L Outer Marker, altitude 2200 feet, speed 250 Knots.

- When ILS glideslope indicator shows 2 dots low – Start descent, accelerating to 350 knots. Arrive over runway end at 40 feet radio altitude.

- Make 350 knot 40 feet high-speed pass over runway 24L.

- At runway end, turn to heading 280°, establish 45° climb, Both Engine Fuel Control Levers - OFF. Perform right aileron roll.

- Lower nose to 10°, start left 45° bank turn, when airspeed reaches 250 knots, extend slats.

- Align with runway 06R. When landing is assured, lower landing gear. Manage energy to touch down between exits AA and Z at 120 knots, 28° flaps.

- Exit runway on high-speed exit Y, turn right and park at Gate D-10.

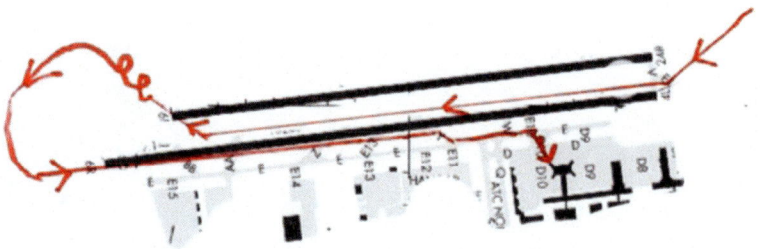

My scribbled LAX Energy Management Finale profile

It worked! The MD-90 handled very well, although the aileron roll was more difficult than I had envisioned – it required a lot of top rudder to keep the nose at 45°. The glider part of the profile was simple energy management: keep airspeed safe, manage altitude control by judicious use of flaps. I had plenty of energy left at touchdown to go all the way to Gate D-10.

During the next few months, I had several late-night FCOM Procedure sessions in the Engineering Simulator. Every time I had a spare 10 minutes, I would practice my LAX Energy Management Finale at different gross weights and speeds. Using good energy management techniques made it possible to make it all the way to Gate D-10 every time. I was lucky:

I heard a story that Bob Hoover once ended his Energy Management Finale 10 feet short of his spot at the crowd line. Embarrassed, he put on his hat, got out of the airplane, and pushed the Aero Commander the remaining 10 feet before he took his bows. I don't think I have the energy to push a MD-90 10 feet!

DO NOT TRY THIS AT HOME, Kids! OR ON THE AIRPLANE! This was just a flight simulator demonstration that even if the unthinkable happens (such as a double engine failure), you will survive if you wisely manage your available energy to FLY THE AIRPLANE

Japan Air System MD-80
"Seven Samurai" paint design by Japanese filmmaker Akira Kurosawa 1910 - 1998

I'll have to admit I used a similar Energy Management challenge on one of my students. Former Apollo 12 Astronaut Pete Conrad (1930-1999) was hired by McDonell Douglas as an Executive Vice President. He was assigned to go on a round-the-world MD-80 marketing tour using a brand-new Muse Air MD-80 and Muse Air cabin crew.

Pete Conrad

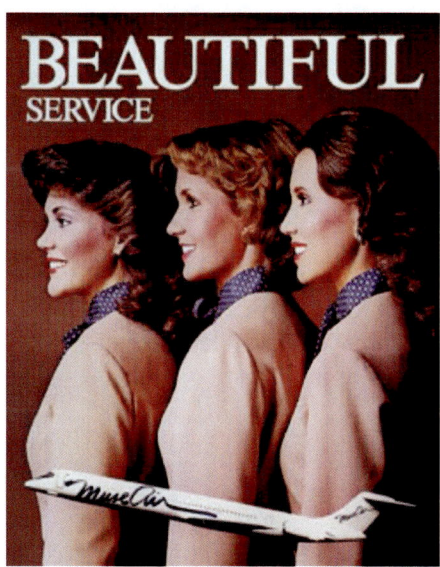

Muse Air – Class Act!

I was assigned to train Pete for a MD-80 Type Rating so he could market the airplane as a rated MD-80 pilot. My boss told me not to baby him, so I gave him everything in the Captains Training Program syllabus plus a few extras not in the training program including a dual flameout (MD-80 Glider!) landing.

Pete handled everything flawlessly. He was an excellent student who studied hard, was prepared for any emergency I confronted him with. And best of all he FLEW THE AIRPLANE! He later told me that I had tested him to the limits of his abilities - He said he hadn't worked that hard in astronaut training! That made me feel good.

Muse Air MD-80

CHAPTER 12:

BUT HE RETIRED IN 2001!

IT'S 2022 - DO YOU STILL HAVE TO FLY THE AIRPLANE?

As I was cleaning up the manuscript getting ready to send this book to the Publisher, I suddenly thought "I haven't touched the controls of an airplane in over 21 years"! How will anybody believe this old geezer if he hasn't kept up with all the wonderful advances in Airplanes, Avionics, Air Traffic Control Procedures and all that other stuff? Since I retired, have they invented some new technology that relieves pilots from their responsibility to FLY THE AIRPLANE?

DOUGLAS MOSS TO THE RESCUE

To my good fortune I have a friend of many years who is still active in flying, and an expert in all things new – Captain Douglas Moss. Doug and I have known each other for over 25 years. The last assignment we had together was in Shenyang, China. We conducted MD-90 Line Training for the pilots of China Northern Airline.

Since then, Doug has wandered into other disciplines, including finishing his Air Force career in the Reserves as an instructor at the USAF Test Pilot School, retiring as a captain at United Airlines, practicing law as an attorney, consulting for various aircraft manufacturers and law firms, and providing flight instruction to owners of pressurized twin-engine aircraft.

CHAPTER 13:

DOUG'S INPUT

CREW RESOURCE MANAGEMENT

"As Charlie Wood points out, CRM started after the 1978 United Airlines Flight 173 accident in Portland, Oregon. Originally entitled Flight Deck Resource Management, which was intended to allow pilots to better communicate with each other, it was enlarged to incorporate other people that pilots must coordinate with, such as flight attendants, dispatchers, and maintenance personnel.

Originally, the two-pilot crews were categorized by the most obvious differentiation, that being who was flying the plane - the Pilot Flying (PF) and the Pilot Not Flying (PNF). This terminology, however, was later changed by acknowledging the PNF's primary duty was to monitor the PF and the whole dynamic flying situation. Thus, the non-flying pilot's title was changed to PM (Pilot Monitoring)".

GLOBAL NAVIGATION SYSTEMS – THE WAY OF THE FUTURE

Global Navigation Satellite System (GNSS) is a general term describing any satellite constellation, such as GPS, that provides positioning, navigation, and timing (PNT) services. Use of GNSS has allowed the FAA to change their airspace management from a VOR Airway centric system to one defined by Performance Based Navigation (PBN). This has become the standard now, rapidly overtaking the use of VOR navigation for pilots. In fact, the FAA has already begun decommissioning many VOR stations, leaving only a few remaining in operation, in case of a GPS outage. This backup concept is called VOR MON (Minimum Operational Network).

Almost all modern or updated aircraft now have GPS receivers and "navigators" or Flight Management Systems that allow the aircraft to fly a pilot-programmed route, without the need for ground-based navigational facilities.

ADS-B COMMUNICATIONS

Automatic Dependent Surveillance-Broadcast (ADS-B) is transforming all segments of aviation. ADS-B provides numerous capabilities, including transmitting the aircraft's position, speed, altitude, heading, and other critical information to Air Traffic Controllers (ATC) and other aircraft without the limitations associated with ATC radar. In addition, it allows weather and traffic information to be transmitted to the aircraft to enhance the pilots' situational awareness. In the future, aircraft will be able to employ both GNSS and ADS-B technology to maintain their own separation between other aircraft when arriving and departing airports.

GPWS AND ITS SUCCESSOR – EGPWS

The original GPWS (Ground Proximity Warning System) had rather limited capability since its only inputs were the aircraft's altitude above the ground (based on the radar altimeter) and the speed and configuration of the plane (position of the gear and flaps). The GPWS system had no idea of where the plane was in the world, thus had no idea where any nearby mountains may lie.

With the advent of the Global Positioning System (GPS) and improved computer processing and data storage, it was possible to calculate the aircraft's position and overlie it in relation to a digitized map of the local terrain. Thus, the computer could anticipate if the aircraft's flight path was directed towards a mountain and could display such terrain to the pilots on the aircraft's Navigation Display (ND) with adequate time to allow the pilots to take evasive action. This *Enhanced* Ground Proximity System (EGPWS) has produced a great improvement in aviation safety.

DATALINK COMMUNICATIONS

A great deal of the advances of the past few decades have revolved around the communications between the pilots and Air Traffic Control (ATC) or the pilot's dispatch. This communication is now done mostly by digital datalink as opposed to voice over the radio. Datalink between the pilots and ATC involves pre-departure clearances (PDC) before takeoff, as well as enroute clearance changes through CPDLC (Controller Pilot Data Link Communications), and ADS-C (Automatic Dependent Surveillance – Contract).

Datalink oceanic clearance

DATALINK ENROUTE WEATHER

For most of aviation's history, the pilot's ability to acquire real-time weather information has been limited to either looking out the window, using voice-radio to talk to a distant meteorologist, or using the aircraft's less-than-optimum onboard radar system. With the advent of satellite communications, however, many airlines have incorporated real-time weather information that includes the aircraft's entire route of flight and allows the pilot to view the graphical color depiction. This has greatly increased the pilots' strategic situational awareness.

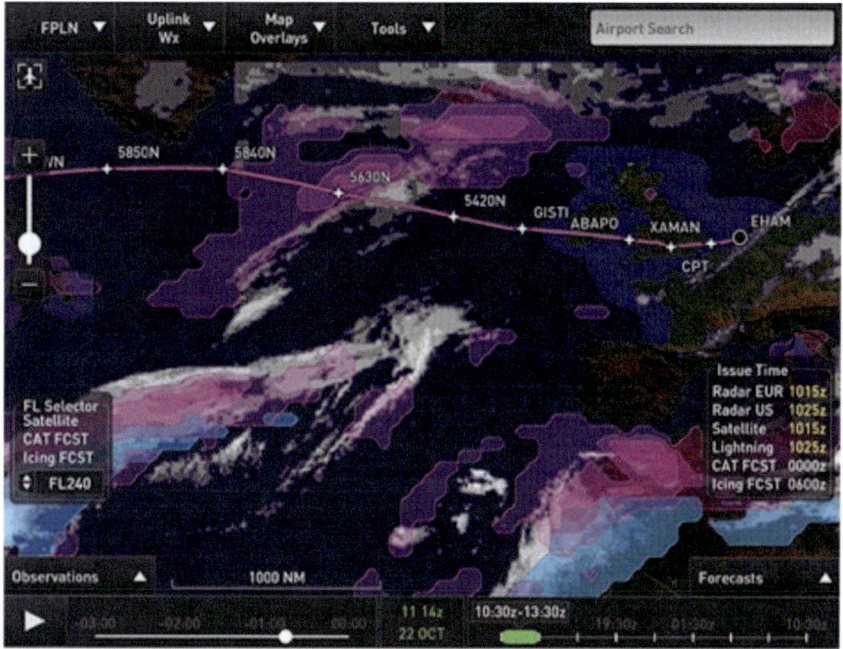

Enroute weather display

INTEGRATED NAVIGATION and VERTICAL DISPLAYS

For most of aviation history, a pilot's navigational displays were devoted primarily to lateral guidance. Although altimeters indicated their vertical position, not much was provided to help the pilot plan and monitor his climbs and descents. Recently, however, a Vertical Situation Display (VSD) has been incorporated by most airliner manufacturers that dramatically increase the pilots' vertical situation awareness - thus allowing them to better FLY THE AIRPLANE.

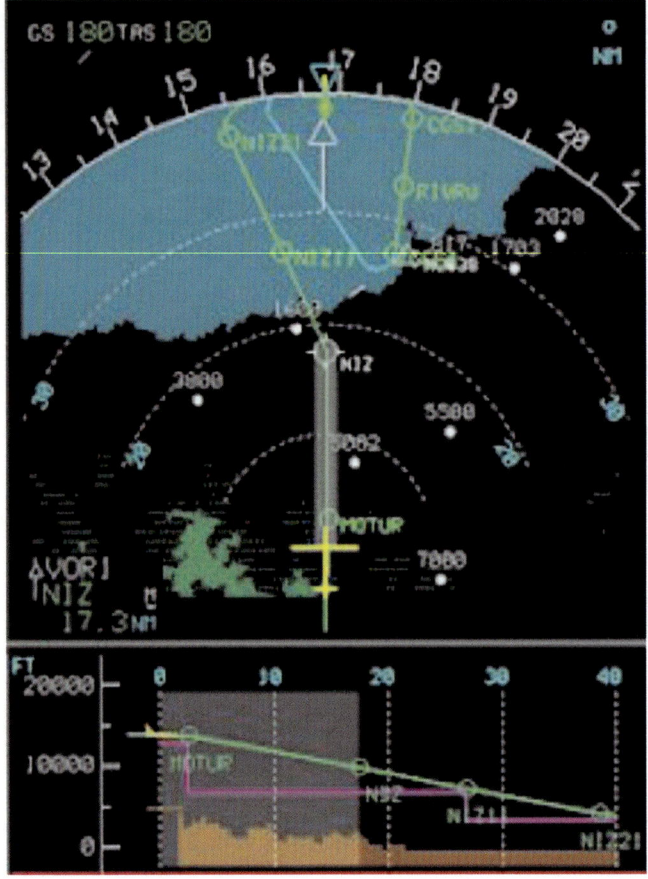

Vertical Situation Display enhances situational awareness

ONBOARD WEATHER RADAR

Modern aircraft radars capitalize on high-speed data processors and digital storage to bring new capabilities to display convective weather to the pilots. Until recently, the pilots had to manually adjust the tilt angle of the radar sweeps and could only view one tilt angle at a time.

Modern radars, however, use their processors to measure 3D-volumetric airspace in multiple tilt scans and then process the combined data into a true 3D representation of the weather ahead of the plane. Additionally, the radar has a digital database of the terrain which is used to reduce the amount of ground return, thus allowing a better display of the actual weather.

Other enhancements include an adaptive weather radar system, one that adapts the weather radar system in accordance with a seasonal parameter, a time-of-day parameter, or a location parameter. This allows the radar to automatically adjust the weather display to respond to the current environment, location, or time in the world where the plane is flying. For example, in the Intertropical Convergence Zone (ITCZ), near the equator, the frequent thunderstorm activity has less water content, which is less reflective to airborne radars. Therefore, when the aircraft is flying in the ITCZ, the radar will automatically increase its gain so that the thunderstorms are more visible to the pilots.

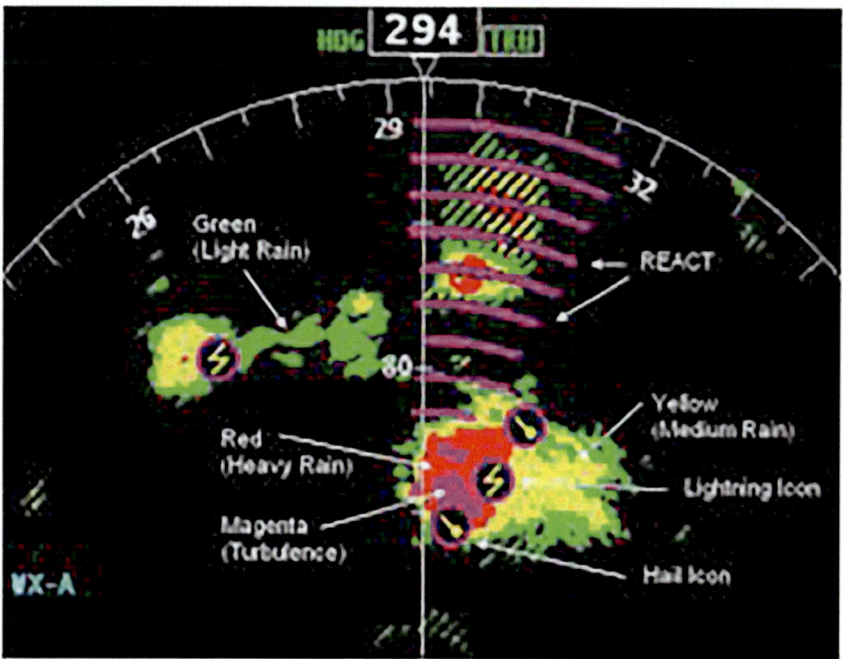

Onboard weather radar

PAPERLESS COCKPIT

At one time, all the paperwork pilots needed for inflight would need to be dragged into the plane by the pilot himself. Those days are now mostly gone. Primarily all documentation now required for flight can be downloaded and carried on a Personal Electronic Device (PED), such as an iPad. Flight Manuals, Flight Plans, Approach Plates, Enroute Charts are all now digitized and incorporated as either genetic documents or processed through proprietary "apps". Although this seems to be a clear improvement in efficiency, it also has produced some unanticipated results. The pilots must be much more tech-savvy to use their PEDs in an efficient and effective way. For "dinosaur" pilots (those old geezers that don't adopt to new technology well), it can be a real challenge.

Use of PEDs in the cockpit (right) now replaces conventional paperwork (left)

CHAPTER 14:

THREE LITTLE WORDS

IT'S NOT THE NUMBER OF WORDS –
IT'S THE WORDS

This isn't a large book because it doesn't take many words to explain the most important thing I learned in my 45 year, 20,000+ flying hour, worldwide accident-free flying career.

In fact, it only takes three words: FLY THE AIRPLANE!

The only reason I wrote this book is to reinforce that these three little words have always had a life or death meaning to someone sitting in or designing a cockpit, and they always will. Statistics have proven that some still don't get it. I want to find these individuals before they do something stupid and kill themselves.

THIS IS A GREAT START!

My nephew Shawn Taylor lives in Fremantle, Australia with his beautiful wife Kell**ie** Patton and their two young boys Sid and Alby.

For as long as I can remember, Shawn has wanted to be a pilot. He admired my brother Edward and his son Ed Jr. because they both obtained their Private Pilot licenses. Because I spent 45 years as a professional pilot, he always considered me his aviation guru.

After Shawn's yoga studio Yogalab Fremantle became a successful business, he decided to fulfill his lifelong dream of obtaining a pilot license. He asked me for advice. I told Shawn that in my opinion he would gain a great advantage as a pilot if he first learned how to FLY THE AIRPLANE by obtaining a private Glider Pilot license. Unfortunately, the nearest glider training facility was too far away to be practical.

Fortunately for Shawn, he found a Flight Instructor who is well versed in the FLY THE AIRPLANE philosophy. I have never met him but listening to Shawn describe his instructional style, I thought he was talking about me!

Dave Schneiker, CFI Royal Aero Club WA, I salute you for your professionalism. You are setting the high standards that will mold my nephew Shawn Taylor into the lifetime safe pilot he must be. I only ask you one favor: I promise to foot the bill if you will take Shawn for an aerotow to 4,000 feet in a sailplane and allow him to experience what it is *really* like to FLY THE AIRPLANE!

I was in the process of writing FLY THE AIRPLANE! when Shawn started his flying lessons. I immediately sent him my draft of the book and insisted that he give it some thought before he ever put his hands and feet on a set of flight controls. He did.

Shawn soloed this year on his mom's (My baby sister's) birthday, and recently sent me his observations. I think he is getting the picture:

"Uncle Charles,

Here's a little info on my FLY THE AIRPLANE experience as a student pilot. I think it's important to address the student pilots on what it means to the FLY THE AIRPLANE in the early phases of training.

FLY THE AIRPLANE!

Pre-Solo. For the student pilot. Learning to fly is one of the most exhilarating, challenging and rewarding pursuits that anyone can imagine. Taking to the sky and entering the 3-d world of the X, Y and Z axis takes some time to learn and with practice begins to take shape even in the early hours of your training.

As a student pilot, pre solo, you are learning all the basics of FLYING THE AIRPLANE and the main thing you need to remember is that the airplane is going to do what you tell it to do. Feeling the effects of controls at all the various airspeeds is critical to the student pilot to develop a sense of connection to the airplane. Airspeed is king.

Your instructor will help you manage the workload in the early phases of flight so you can stay focused on FLYING THE AIRPLANE. They'll help you with radio communication and navigation until you're ready to take these on yourself.

You need to FLY THE AIRPLANE. Learning your airspeeds and learning to trim the airplane allow you to relax and enjoy what you're doing. Learning by hearing different rpms and power setting changes without looking at your tachometer keeps your eyes out of the cockpit. Learning all your attitude sight pictures by looking at the horizon gives you 90% of the information you need. Your instruments are always there to verify what you see.

Even before you start the airplane as a student pilot, look at each instrument to familiarize yourself with their placement and learn to scan before you even put the keys in the ignition and begin your pre-start checks. You want that cockpit to feel like home.

There were so many instances in my pre solo training where my instructor told me to FLY THE AIRPLANE. If the airplane wasn't trimmed and a radio call came in, if I tried to answer that call my instructor would stop me before I made it and would make me trim the airplane first and then call.

Another scenario was during my first few circuit lessons I would ask for feedback on my landings, and he would keep his mouth shut until we were well into our upwind climb out, he would take the controls and then give me feedback when it was safe to do so. FLY THE AIRPLANE. He drilled these habits into my flying early on and it's become instinctual to "Aviate" first. Creating good habits early is critical to being a safe pilot.

First solo. I knew my first solo was coming up soon. As my pattern work improved and my instructor said less as we flew laps around the airfield. Like many student pilots I had a tremendous amount of anxiety around becoming PIC without the safety net of my instructor.

Good CFIs know when their student is ready before the student may feel ready for that first big milestone in their training. When that day finally comes and your instructor gets out it's the most exciting, terrifying, gratifying feeling ever. A moment that every student pilot anticipates and a moment no pilot ever forgets. Everything you've learned gets put to the test.

Shawn and a Cessna 152 Aerobat

Shawn and CFI Dave Schneiker

It's easy to get lost in the fear of all the things that could go wrong. There are You Tube videos of student pilots crashing on their first solo. The one thing I had ingrained in my head from the moment my instructor got out was FLY THE AIRPLANE, no matter what happens, even if I lost my engine, I knew I'd immediately push the yoke forward and pitch the Cessna 152 to best glide - 65knots. I know from practice that three swipes down on the trim wheel will put the 152 right at 65 knots.

I knew that even if I couldn't find a suitable area to land, I will take Bob Hoover's advice and FLY THE AIRPLANE all the way into the crash. I know that if I don't go into an aerodynamic stall my chances of walking away increase. I know that the more I slow the airplane down just before impact, the less energy you bring into the crash. FLY THE AIRPLANE all the way through. It's easy to see how a student pilot could freak out and stop FLYING THE AIRPLANE but there are also numerous You Tube videos out there that show student pilots landing safely in engine out scenarios through staying calm, focused and simply FLYING THE AIRPLANE."

Shawn, even though you said ". . . even if I couldn't find a suitable area to land, I will take Bob Hoover's advice and FLY THE AIRPLANE . . ." instead of saying ". . . even if I couldn't find a suitable area to land, I will take Uncle Charles' advice and FLY THE AIRPLANE . . .", I forgive you for taking Bob Hoover's advice instead of Uncle Charles' - because you used the three most important words you need to use as a pilot: FLY THE AIRPLANE!

MY DESIRED IMPACT OF THIS BOOK

My audience is very small. If you count every wannabe pilot, student pilot, professional or private pilot (civilian, military, fixed or rotary wing, glider/sailplane, tiny single-seat propeller plane or jumbo jet) and every airplane manufacturer or design engineer in the world, you are only talking about less than three million people. These people are rare in our society because *all* of them routinely *read* and *understand* written materials such as flight manuals or design specs, instead of spending all day fixated on their smart phones. It takes less than a day to read this book.

I deliberately published this book in paperback and eBook format to keep the cost low and reach the maximum number of people in my target audience; I sincerely feel that my message is much more important than money. My hope is that someone in my target group will read the paperback, like it and pass it on to another. Hopefully it will become required pre–flight reading in learning institutions with flying programs such as the U.S. Air Force Academy, the University of North Dakota, Embry-Riddle Aeronautical University and others.

If anyone who reads this book finds themselves in a cockpit where no one is FLYING THE AIRPLANE and thinks "That old pilot Charlie Wood warned me about this, so I'd better FLY THE AIRPLANE!" and if that saves one or more lives, I will be an incredibly happy person.

FLY THE AIRPLANE!

MISSION COMPLETE!
Charlie Wood